CONTENT

Accelerate YOUR SUCCESS

INDIE SINGERS & SONGWRITERS

BEEBY LEIGH

Accelerate Your Success Indie Singers and Songwriters

DEDICATION

To my daughter Brooke
You are my greatest teacher, love and inspiration.

To my mum Lynda
For showing me determination to never give up, and for
being my "constant" throughout my life.

INTRODUCTION

Welcome to the start of an amazing discovery

Hello, thank you, and Congratulations, on purchasing "Accelerate Your Success Indie Singers & Songwriters" to help take your hobby or career, and your life to the next level.

"I Am Super Excited For You"

Now, before we jump in, a few things to note. Do not do comparison-itis, this journey is about you and nobody else. You have this book for life. So that you can come back to the content again and again.

If you read this entire book without skipping ahead, and do the work within it, go at your own pace, allow yourself to be open and curious to new ideas, then accelerated success in your career and life is yours for the taking.

As you go through the book, I will explain different techniques that help to reframe what you are seeing in your reality and identify things that have been hidden in your energy, and help you to dissolve them in the most easiest, and effortless way.

You will be given specific techniques or quantum questions to help assist you in tapping into your energy to discover what is hidden, so that you can at last figure out what has been eluding you from success thus far.

I don't consider myself religious or spiritual, so this book is not based on energy woo-woo. All the techniques are certified, and backed by psychology, science and/or neuroscience based discoveries on human behaviour, and energy & mindset alignment.

The fact that you are reading these introductory words tells me a few things about you. Firstly, it suggests that you aspire to live an extraordinary life and are willing to make changes to your current circumstances.

Furthermore, it implies that you have already invested time, energy, and resources into creating the life you desire, however you may still have some unresolved issues.

Perhaps certain aspects of your life are still unsatisfying, or maybe your current life is already great, yet you are looking for ways to take it to the next level. Perhaps, like me, and many of my clients you have faced a challenging or traumatic childhood, or life, and its effects still linger in certain areas of your life or career. You may have tried various solutions that promise to improve your life, but have yet to find lasting relief.

Like many, you may have acknowledged that you play a role in shaping your life, yet are uncertain about how you have been doing so unconsciously, and how to start doing it intentionally. You may have invested a lot of time, energy, and money in self-help and personal development, yet still feel stuck.

Please know that you are not broken, or unlucky and you are capable of creating the life you want. In this book, I reveal how you are currently creating your life, how to stop doing it unconsciously, and how to start doing it intentionally to ultimately lead you to complete personal-financial freedom.

You'll Discover

- Exactly how you are creating your life as it is
- How to stop doing it by default
- How to END the endless self-help loop of hope, purchase, disappointment, hope…
- And how to begin to consciously, intentionally create the Success, Happiness, Wealth, Relationships, and life you desire
- How to step into Total Personal-Financial Freedom

If you have felt confused, unclear, frustrated or disappointed in how to actually do this, I want you to know that I can relate and I understand. This book may just be the thing to finally end your search. Before my breakthrough that set me free and that inspired me to write this book, my "previous life" was a wreck, a string of disasters, including a divorce, multiple "failed" relationships, huge amounts of debt nearly costing me my home, and depression that nearly derailed my singing career, when I started suffering with stage fright and memory loss of lyrics to songs.

During much of my life, I felt a combination of severe loss, rejection, abandonment, anger and depression and for several years, the thought of "what's the point of being here" was my ever present companion. After many years of disappointing self-help options, I discovered, healed and became advanced certified in six different energy alignment techniques and music therapy to radically transform my life, and to help others that were not living the life they envisioned.

The main idea behind my work and this book is to shift you from creating unconsciously by default to intentionally using infinite energy to create the life you desire through conscious effort.

As I previously mentioned, the fact that you are reading this book suggests that you are aware or have an inkling that you are responsible for shaping your life. It's likely that you have been doing so unconsciously or at best, with only partial awareness.

In this book, I will clearly and thoroughly demonstrate how to start intentionally creating the success, wealth, relationships, and life you desire. I will provide guidance on how to do this in every aspect of your life with complete understanding.

Consciously creating your life as a singer or songwriter means consciously taking control of your energy, thoughts, emotions, and actions, and aligning them with your desires. It is about being aware of your thoughts, emotions, beliefs, programming, conditioning, fears, hidden blocks and inactions and making conscious choices to move towards your desires both limitlessly and fearlessly.

As I discovered along my journey, only focusing on mindset changes, vision boards or visualisations does not "dissolve" your past programming, conditioning, traumas or fears. However, by ulitising both energy alignment and mindset techniques, you can achieve lasting transformational change rather than a temporary fix that many self-help and personal development companies try to sell you.

Throughout this book I reference the word "trauma" within our energy. Please note that the meaning of the word in relation to this book, is the "impact on our energy through our perceptions of events, words, thoughts, beliefs and emotions" and it does not mean that you could have severe trauma like PTSD. However, the techniques shown can help with both mild and severe trauma that maybe held within your energy.

****

Intension Setting

Before you embark on this journey, it's important to get clear about your intention for reading this book. You've undoubtedly come here with a desire to level up your success game, but this journey will be unique to each individual.

Take a moment to write down what you hope to achieve by reading this book. Don't worry if it seems unachievable at this moment; as you progress through these pages, you will come to realise that there are infinite possibilities and that you can align your energy with them.

CHAPTER ONE
My Story...then and now

For years I hid my story in shame believing it had no value to anyone. Patterns of imposter syndrome and judgement arose every time I tried to explain, why I had developed stage fright, memory loss of lyrics and money issues after years of being ok.

On reflection, I realised by telling you my story it was not to bore you, but to enable you to see how our life experiences impact our energy, our thoughts, our beliefs, and our emotions, and how they imbed into every area of our lives to impact our present, even when we believe they have no relevance to what we are currently experiencing.

My desire is to make an impact on millions of singers and songwriters lives around the globe with this book. However, even if I only managed to help a handful of people become free from whatever blocks hold them back in life, then my perception, and my truth is well worth telling.

To the human eye I had a privileged life, that's true. I certainly couldn't say my childhood was a bad one, as I always had a roof over my head, food on the table, warmth and love. It was full of happy memories, a mum that was always there supporting and loving me, a circle of great friends, that I am eternally grateful for. Yet to invisible eyes rejection, abandonment, loss and failure wounds ran so deeply, plaguing my emotions, actions and my reactions for nearly 40yrs. Making me believe I was not good enough, loveable or deserving enough, and subconsciously reflecting all of this into my reality repeatedly, to not enable me to be successful, abundant or loved.

"I know exactly what I want to be when I grow up!!"

My grandparents on both sides of the family lived in West Sussex, UK not far from the beach, less than a mile from each other. From the time I was 4yrs old when my parents divorced, my brother and I would stay with both sets of grandparents through the school holidays, as my mum and dad both worked full time.

I was always a dreamer, and loved to sing, around the house, in the car, and junior school choir. I would get my brother who is 16 months older than me to hold the microphone above my head, while I pretended to play guitar of which I couldn't play a note at the time, and take pictures in our living room as if I was on stage.

The day I announced to the universe what I desired in life it was 1982, and I was 7yrs old. I remember the day vividly like it was yesterday, it was the Easter holidays, and I was staying at my mum's parent's house 'Little Nan and Little Grandad' as they were affectionately known, for the week.

This particular day we'd come home from a walk along the seafront, and my nan & I were snugged on their two seater sofa, watching the film about the life of Tammy Wynette, the famous America country singer. I remember being in absolute awe at the end scene of the movie where Tammy Wynette's character, receives a standing ovation for singing 'Stand By Your Man' at the Grand Ole Opry in Nashville.

In that moment, the emotion of the scene hit a chord with my heart, as the characters face was of complete shock that so many people were supporting her dream.

I stood up, proudly puffed out my chest and announced…

"Nan and the world, I know exactly what I want to be when I grow up!!". *"What is that then my love"* Little Nan said.

Without any doubt in my voice, I said:

> *"I want to become a famous singer, and sing my own songs live at the Grand Ole Opry, in front of an audience of fans that love me as much as that lady"*

From that day on it was high up on my intentional bucket list to achieve one day, yet my journey created years of doubting and judging myself and feeling judged by others, that I started asking the universe "Am I even worthy of my dreams becoming reality?".

My Rejection, Abandonment, & Loss
(Energy Blocks)

My Grandad: During my childhood, I was rejected on a regular basis by my grandad. He would use money as a bargaining tool for affection, and I always felt like I was auditioning to be his granddaughter. He would lavish my brother with expensive gifts, take him abroad on holiday without me, allow him to stay up late while making me go to bed early. I would hear them whispering loudly and cracking jokes from my bedroom, and constantly praising him on every little thing. My brother and I were close siblings yet their unequal treatment was infuriating, and I resented the fact my brother was treated differently.

My mind constantly asking "what's wrong with me, why does he not love me the same?". The pattern of people pleasing in the hope that I could gain his love and attention began.

I was 11 years old, when my grandad was diagnosed with pancreatic cancer he went downhill rapidly, and had passed within 6 weeks of the diagnosis. I was sad when he passed, as despite his actions I loved him very much, and the hope of receiving his unconditional love, died along with him.

My Dad: Even though I was only 4yrs old when my parents separated, I had always idolised him. From a distance my parents seemed amicable, yet by the time I was 8yrs old they were constantly attending court over money, custody or disagreeing on schools. I felt like a pawn in a game of chess. At this point I was about to move to school number 4. The pattern of loss had became a regular occurrence, as I'd form friendships that I never got the chance to develop before moving onto the next school. Then suddenly, my dad would turn up weeks after our birthdays and Christmases without presents, and he'd miss school plays and events, which was totally out of character to the dad he had once been.

In the same year my grandad died of cancer, my mum gave birth to my younger sister, I started high school, and my dad got remarried. Shortly after my dad moved house and within the blink of an eye, they were no longer in our lives at all. No forwarding address, no more phone calls, and no explanation to why.

I was 24 years old the first time I saw or heard from my Dad again, yet within less than a year I endured abandonment and rejection all over again.

I was determined not to show the world I was affected by his choice. Internally, it had knocked my confidence and validated the beliefs I already had about myself from my grandad; *"You, are not worthy, you are not good enough, your voice is not valid, showing vulnerability is a negative thing, and don't trust anyone."*

****

Not Worthy Money, Love, Success (Energy Blocks)

To the outside world I was confident and happy, and people seemed to like me. Yet in my inner world I felt worthless, like I didn't matter, that I wasn't good enough for my dreams to become reality. This felt like it changed when I met the man I would marry. Emigrated to Vancouver, Canada and got my first big singing break. The trouble with happy ever after when you don't believe you deserve it, is at some point the sticky plaster masking the insecurities will come off subconsciously validating your belief that you're not worthy all over again.

When I emigrated to Canada in 2001, I signed up for some singing lessons as a way to meet new people. My teacher Kimberley encouraged me to enter provincial competitions, talent shows, yet it wasn't until 2004 that my big break happened. It was while hosting a VIP event for Labatt Breweries the company I worked for at the time, at the Merritt Mountain Music Festival, a slightly smaller country music version of Glastonbury. I asked the lead singer of a well-known local band if I could sing a song with them on the main stage in front of thousands of people. To be honest I thought they would say no, as they had no clue if I could even sing. Instead, Ken McCoy the lead singer handed me the mic and said "what song would you like us to play?".

It wasn't Nashville or the Grand Ole Opry, yet in that moment it felt like the universe was finally giving me my dream. It felt amazing, and the buzz of being on a huge stage in front of thousands of people singing live for the first time was phenomenal. The crowd cheered and asked for more, and from there on I got to sing at that festival, and with that band several years running.

"I'm A Failure" (Energy Blocks)

Several years into my marriage we started trying for kids, but never fell pregnant. Of course I blamed myself even though there was no evidence to prove that theory. Finally after nearly 3 years and 3 rounds of full IVF - I fell pregnant!! Yay!! To say we were over the moon would be an understatement. We went for the 12 weeks scan and everything seemed normal, excitedly we delivered the news to our friends and family. Two weeks later I miscarried. We were devastated, yet we never really spoke about it again.

The pressure was intense as now everyone was invested in us falling pregnant. I was petrified of more heartache, and I didn't think I could try again. For months I ponded on what to do, until finally, I proceeded with IVF number 4. In 2010, after a long labour and emergency C-section. Our daughter was born healthy, adorable and perfect. I was in love.

This happiness was short lived as severe post-partum depression hit me like a freight train. I didn't recognise the signs at first, as I thought exhaustion, endless crying and feeling like I couldn't cope with anything, even getting out of bed was normal. It wasn't until a neighbour, who'd gone through a similar experience years before noticed the signs and then my doctor confirmed the diagnoses.

I barely recognised myself in the mirror anymore, my world felt dark and nothing I tried seemed to help. I was pushing people away out of shame as I was embarrassed I couldn't cope on my own, and judged and compared myself to others and new mums. I felt like an absolute failure.

Depression engulfed me further, I felt guilty and ashamed that I had let everyone down, especially my daughter who'd have to grow up in separate houses, when my husband and I separate a year later. I had let my fears, abandonment triggers, and deep depression contribute to the failure of my marriage.

Life Changing Choice
(Dissolved Energy Blocks)

I suffered depression for many years, until 2016 when a friend introduced me to energy alignment modalities. To say I was sceptical would be an understatement, but at that point I was willing to try any means to get my life and singing career back on track. As singing live for a couple of years had resulted in panic attacks, stage fright and memory loss to lyrics of songs, even songs I'd sung a million times before.

Not only did I completely dissolve all depression, stage fright, visibility issues and memory loss issues, I also dissolved phobias and allergies that I'd suffered with since childhood. As they were all linked to the same traumas, fears, emotions and beliefs that I'd had held in my energy.

I knew then and there, that it was my purpose to help other people live their lives free from blocks holding them back from success too. So, I took a leap of faith on myself and left my corporate job that I'd always done alongside my singing career, and invest in all the necessary training and certifications to become a transformational change expert, energy & mindset alignment mentor, and I learnt how to write my own songs to create the life I had envisioned as a child.

In Oct 2016, I launched my first debut single and won an international award that same year. In early 2017 I started my company Transform Like Butterflies (that later changed to Beeby Leigh Music), a transformational change, energy alignment, and life coaching company helping people accelerate success within their career, personal life, and finances using energy alignment techniques.

In 2020 at the start of the first lockdown of the pandemic, I started receiving more and more client enquiries from the music industry. I was becoming the number one choice for my ideal clients. By the end of the first lockdown, I renamed my company to my artist & author name to capture my talents of singing, songwriting and mentoring all under one brand name, and realigned my client base to solely working with music industry professionals. And, In October 2020 I even had the honour of mentoring my first celebrity client, who was emotionally struggling with the shutdown of her tour and life converting to a virtual world.

Testimonial

Working with Beeby Leigh catapulted me into a different realm of thinking. I had never participated in any type of life coaching or energy alignment work before, so I wasn't sure how effective it would be for me. During our sessions, I began to see radical changes in my life. Things that I desired were starting to come to fruition. I learned that the energy that I put out has a direct correlation to what I will receive.
David Moreton – Singer-Songwriter - New York, USA

Have a question for me?
Ask by visiting www.beebyleighmusic.com.
I'd love to hear from you

EXERCISE ONE

Open Yourself UP With A "Two Question" Technique

Now you know my story. that I was in hell and energy alignment changed everything. And you know my promise with this book is to help you to have the same experience.

Here are two questions to help you more fully open yourself up to the information that I am about to share with you.

Please breathe deeply, and take a moment to really feel each question, and the energies that arise in your body in response.

- "How would I feel if I were totally free in every area of life?"

- "How would I feel if I had infinite power, limitless guidance, and the emotional presence to navigate every life situation with ease and grace?"

Take a moment to really FEEL the energies in your body responding to those two questions. Suspend your doubts and **Lets dive in….**

CHAPTER TWO
"What is Energy Alignment?"

Our Energy is complex, yet simple put "Energy Alignment" refers to the alignment of one's thoughts, emotions, beliefs and actions with one's desires and values. It is the process of aligning your energy with what you truly desire and making sure that your thoughts, emotions, beliefs and actions are in sync with your desires. When you are in alignment, you are able to tap into your full potential and achieve success.

Energy alignment can be achieved through a variety of techniques, which I will show you throughout this book. These techniques will not be the usual meditation, affirmations, visalisations, vision boards, or "think positive" strategies, that many other self help experts promote.

Practicing the techniques within this book can help you to raise your vibration, dissolve thoughts, beliefs and emotions that are not serving you, and align your energy with your desires, and values.

If you want to achieve success in the music industry, or the sync licensing industry, your thoughts, emotions and actions should be in energetic alignment with those desires, and values. Your thoughts and feeling should be energetically aligned to motivate and inspire you, to take the necessary actions that will lead you to your goals and desires.

"What could be the long term affects for Singers and Songwriters if they are out of energetic alignment?"

Being out of energetic alignment can have a variety of negative effects on singers and songwriters. It can lead to a lack of inspiration and creativity, as well as difficulty in connecting with the emotions and messages in your music. It can also lead to physical strain on the vocal cords, and difficulty in performing. Additionally, being out of energetic alignment can cause emotional and mental stress, which can negatively impact overall well-being. It is important for singers and songwriters to take care of their physical, emotional, and spiritual well-being in order to maintain alignment and continue to create meaningful and impactful music.

It's important to note that energy alignment is not a one-time event, it's a continuous process throughout your life. As we go through different stages in our lives, we may encounter new challenges, obstacles, and opportunities that can cause us to lose alignment. That's why it's important to regularly check in with yourself and make sure that your energy is aligned with your goals, desires, and values.

Our Reality Is A Reflection

Our reality is a reflection of our fears, emotions, beliefs, traumas, decisions, and conclusions. This means that the way we perceive and experience the world is shaped by our internal state, including our thoughts, emotions, and beliefs.

For Example: If someone has a fear of failure, they may hold themselves back from taking risks and pursuing opportunities. As a result, they may not achieve the success they desire. On the other hand, if someone has a belief in their own abilities and a positive attitude, they may be more likely to take risks and achieve success.

Emotions also play a role in shaping our reality. If we perceive emotions such as fear, anger, and resentment as negative we create a negative reality, while if we perceive emotions such as love, joy, and gratitude we create a positive reality.

Traumas and past experiences can also shape our reality. These experiences can create limiting beliefs and negative patterns of behaviour that can affect our current actions and decisions.

Decisions and conclusions also shape our reality. The choices we make, and the beliefs we hold can affect the outcomes of our experiences and shape our perception of the world.

It's important to note that this perspective is not universally accepted and other perspectives may hold that reality is not solely a reflection of our internal state, but also influenced by external factors, such as the physical and social environment. However, many people find that understanding and working with their internal state can be beneficial for their personal growth and well-being.

"How Does Our Belief System Work?"

As humans, we develop our beliefs, patterns, and emotions before we are 7 years old. This is generally due to our interactions with our parents and other caregivers.

For Example: If our parents are always stressed out and never take the time to relax, we will likely develop the belief that life is always stressful. This will then cause us to act in a way that is consistent with this belief (e.g., being constantly in fear or stressed), which will likely lead to negative emotions like sadness, anger etc.

Our beliefs, patterns and emotions develop during our early years, and it has been proven that even as early as while in the womb. We learn how to interact with the world around us through the examples that our caregivers provide.

For Example: If a child is constantly yelled at or punished for making mistakes, they will start to believe that they are not good enough. This can lead to low self-esteem and things like depression in later life. Alternatively, if a child is praised for their efforts, they will learn that it is okay to make mistakes and that they can always try again. This will help them to have a positive outlook on life, be more resilient and take risks.

Our beliefs and patterns of behaviour are also developed through interactions with our peers.

For Example: If a child is constantly bullied at school, they may start to believe that they are not good enough or that they are worthless. This can lead to social anxiety and isolation in later life. Alternatively, if a child has friends who support them and accept them for who they are, they will learn that it is okay to be different and that they are loved and valued. This will help them to have a positive self-image and be more confident in themselves.

Different Layers of Beliefs and Feelings

The Core Level: Is what we are taught and accept from childhood in this lifetime. They are beliefs that have become part of us. Energetically they are held as energy in the frontal lobe of the brain.

The Genetic Level: This includes programme's passed onto us from our ancestors, or are added to our genes in this life. These beliefs are energies stored in the morphogenetic field around our physical DNA. This energy tells the DNA what to do. Energetically this is around the pineal gland.

Collective Consciousness Level - This includes memories from past lives, parallel lives, deep genetic memories or collective consciousness experiences that we carry into the present moment. These memories are held in our auric field around the back of the neck and shoulders. Think of the collective consciousness belief programme's coming through because of us all being part of the one big electromagnetic field and therefore interconnected.

The Soul Level - Here the belief programme's are held at soul level, and energetically begin at the heart chakra and moving out through the layers of the aura.

A belief or feeling may be on one level only, or it may be on more. Equally we may have two counter opposing beliefs or dual beliefs (such as I love myself and I hate myself, we may have both).

"What could the long term affects for Singers and Songwriters be if trauma or emotions were left undetected in one or more of the levels?"

If trauma or emotions are left unresolved at deep levels, such as the core, genetic, collective conscious, or soul levels, they may cause an individual to be out of energetic alignment. This can manifest in a variety of ways, including physical and emotional symptoms. In the case of singers and songwriters, unresolved trauma or emotions may affect their ability to create and perform music. They may struggle with writer's block, stage fright, or difficulty connecting with their audience. Additionally, unresolved trauma or emotions may manifest in the lyrics and themes of their music, potentially impacting the emotional response of listeners. It is important for singers and songwriters to address any unresolved trauma or emotions in order to maintain their well-being and continue to create meaningful and authentic art.

Energy Bodies

Energy bodies refer to the various layers of energy that exist around and within our physical body. These energy bodies are connected to our physical, emotional, mental and spiritual (Universal) well-being. The concept of energy bodies is based on the belief that everything in the universe is made up of energy, including living beings.

There are several different types of energy bodies, but some of the most commonly recognised energy bodies include:

The Physical Body: This is the most tangible and visible layer of energy that makes up our physical body. It includes all the organs, bones, muscles, and tissues that make up our physical form.

The Emotional Body: This layer of energy is associated with our emotions and feelings. It is believed to be connected to our ability to experience and express emotions, and can affect our overall well-being.

The Mental Body: This layer of energy is associated with our thoughts, beliefs, and perceptions. It is believed to be connected to our ability to think, reason, and make decisions, and can affect our overall well-being.

The Spiritual (Universal) Body: This layer of energy is associated with our connection to a higher power, inner wisdom, and sense of purpose. It is believed to be connected to our ability to experience spiritual transcendence and inner Peace.

There are additional layers such as the etheric body, the astral body, and the causal body, but for the purpose of this book, we will focus on these main 4 energy bodies.

"What could be the long term affects for Singers and Songwriters if trauma or emotions were left undetected in the energy bodies?"

If a person has unresolved trauma or emotions in their energy bodies, it can lead to energetic imbalances that can affect their physical, emotional, and mental well-being. For singers and songwriters, this can manifest in a number of ways, including difficulty accessing their full range of vocal expression, difficulty connecting with their creative impulses, and difficulty expressing themselves authentically in their music. Additionally, unresolved emotional issues can also lead to performance anxiety and stage fright. It's important to address these issues to allow for full expression in one's artistic pursuits.

Energy System Structures

As energy blocks get hidden in your energy system structures, as well as your head, heart, hara, chakras and meridians, this book will show you how to dissolve hidden blocks from all of these areas.

Cellular System Structure: Refers to the physical structure and organisation of cells in the body. It is the basic unit of life and is responsible for carrying out all the functions necessary for the survival of the organism to keep the body functioning properly.

If a singer or songwriter's cellular system structure is out of alignment or blocked from carrying out necessary functions, it could have a significant impact on their ability to perform. Physical symptoms such as pain, fatigue, and illness can affect a person's energy level, stamina, and overall health, making it difficult to sing, perform or connect with an audience during performances. Additionally, negative emotions such as depression or unresolved emotional traumas can affect a person's mood and ability to express themselves creatively, making it difficult to write or perform music.

For Singers: An out of alignment cellular system structure could affect their vocal cords, making it harder to produce clear and powerful sounds, or it could lead to hoarseness or other voice problems.

For Songwriters: It could affect their ability to focus and generate new ideas, leading to difficulty in writing or composing new music.

It is important for singers and songwriters to take care of their physical and mental well-being in order to maintain optimal health and performance. This can include getting enough sleep, eating healthily, and getting regular fresh air and exercise – even if that's just taking a walk.

DNA System Structure: Is a double helix, made up of two strands of nucleotides that run in opposite directions and are held together by hydrogen bonds between complementary base pairs (adenine-thymine and cytosine-guanine). The sequence of these bases carries the genetic information that determines the characteristics of an organism.

"How could this affect Singers and Songwriters if their DNA system structure was out of alignment or blocked from undetected trauma or emotions?"

This could cause changes in gene expression or other alterations in the DNA system structure, it could potentially have a negative impact on the individual's physical and mental health over time. It could affect the individual's vocal cords or other parts of the body used in singing. Similarly, conditions such as depression and fear (anxiety), which are associated with changes in the brain resulting from chronic stress, could affect an individual's ability to write or perform music or lead to various health issues, such as cardiovascular disease, diabetes, and cancer, which could affect the physical ability to sing and perform. This is a complex topic that requires a multidisciplinary approach to be fully understood, which would probably take another full book to explain. However; for the purpose of this book you do not need to understand any of the energy system structures in depth for you to dissolve what is hidden within them.

Just being conscious that these are areas to check is all that you need to know.

Nervous System Structure: The nervous system is a complex network of nerves and cells that transmit signals between different parts of the body. It is divided into two main parts: The central nervous system (CNS) and the peripheral nervous system (PNS). The CNS consists of the brain and spinal cord, while the PNS consists of all the nerves that extend out from the brain and spinal cord to the rest of the body.

"If there were blocks in the Nervous system structure, what could be the long term affects for Singers and Songwriters?"

This can be detrimental to the career of singers and songwriters, as it can affect their ability to perform and create music.

Physical symptoms: This may include tension or pain in the muscles and joints, stiffness, limited range of motion, and difficulty breathing. These symptoms can affect the singer's voice and performance, making it difficult to sing or play instruments with ease.

Emotional symptoms: This may include anxiety, depression, and other psychological disorders. These conditions can negatively impact one's ability to perform and create music, as well as overall mental and physical well-being. Additionally, blocks in the nervous system structure can also cause difficulty in controlling emotions, lack of motivation, and difficulty in expressing oneself, which can be detrimental for singers and songwriters who need to express their emotions through music.

Head, Heart and Hara Balance

Balancing the energy in the head, heart, and hara (also known as the "tanden" or "dantian" in Chinese and Japanese cultures, respectively) brings a sense of overall well-being and balance to one's physical, emotional, and spiritual health.

"If trauma or emotions were left undetected in the head, heart and hara, what could be the long term affects for Singers and Songwriters?"

This can potentially lead to a variety of negative effects for singers and songwriters. These effects could include difficulty in accessing or expressing emotions in their music, difficulty in performing or writing, and difficulty in connecting with audiences. Additionally, unresolved trauma or emotions can also contribute to physical and mental health issues, such as anxiety, depression, and difficulty in maintaining healthy relationships. In order to prevent these negative effects, it is important for singers and songwriters to address any unresolved trauma or emotions and to work on maintaining emotional and energetic balance within their head, heart and hara.

"How do Singers and Songwriters benefit if their Head, Heart and Hara are aligned and balanced?"

- Improve overall sense of well-being and safety.
- Improve focus and concentration
- Increase feelings of inner peace and tranquility
- Enhance intuition and creativity
- Promote emotional balance and stability

Chakras: Chakras are the energy centers in the body. There are seven main chakras in the body, each located in a different area and associated with different physical, emotional, and spiritual aspects of a person. They are responsible for the flow of energy throughout the body and the balance of different aspects of a person's being.

"How can it affect Singers and Songwriters if their Chakras are not open and spinning in the right direction at the right speed?"

If the chakras are not open and spinning in the right direction at the right speed, it can lead to various physical and emotional imbalances. For singers and songwriters, this can manifest in a number of ways such as difficulty expressing themselves creatively and emotionally, fear of performing, difficulty accessing certain emotions, or vocal range, and stage fright. It can also lead to physical symptoms such as tension or strain in the voice, which can impact the quality of their performances.

The techniques within this book will enable you to dissolve any blocks, to ensure your chakras can be open and spinning in the right direction at the right speed.

Meridians: Meridians are energy channels in the body to balance the flow of Qi (energy) throughout the body. When the flow of Qi is blocked or imbalanced, it can result in physical and emotional symptoms.

In relation to singing and songwriting, if the meridians are not open, expansive and in flow, it may affect the singer's or songwriter's ability to fully express themselves and their emotions, potentially leading to difficulties with vocal technique and creativity.

> *"If trauma or emotions were left undetected or not released from the Meridians what could be the long term affects for Singers and Songwriters?"*

If trauma or emotions are left undetected or not released from the meridians, it can result in blockages or imbalances in the flow of Qi (energy) throughout the body.

Physical symptoms: This can manifest in physical and emotional symptoms such as, difficulty expressing themselves emotionally and creatively while singing or songwriting, difficulty with vocal technique such as difficulty hitting certain notes or maintaining proper breath control.

Emotional symptoms: Emotional and psychological issues such as anxiety, depression, and difficulty connecting with their art and audience. Difficulty with stage presence and performing in front of an audience. Lack of inspiration, motivation, and creativity. It's important to note that these effects can vary depending on the individual and the severity of the trauma or emotions. Additionally, addressing these issues through therapy, energy work, and other self-care practices can help to release blocked emotions and improve overall well-being.

The techniques within this book will enable you to dissolve any and all blocks, to ensure your physical and emotional well-being is in energetic alignment.

Your Energy Is Always In One of Three States

Reversal (Reversed): This is where behaviours and/or emotions can indicate that your energy is out of balance, and going in the complete opposite to your desires.

"How could this affect Singers and Songwriters, if their energy is in reversal (going in the opposite direction to being in flow state)?"

- Difficulty connecting with their emotions and expressing themselves authentically in their music

- Struggles with writer's block or a lack of inspiration

- Difficulty connecting with their audience and building a strong fan-base

- Constant negative self-talk and self-doubt

- Difficulty creating a sense of balance between their personal and professional lives.

- Struggle to access their creative abilities and produce new music, find it difficult to stay focused, or experience a lack of motivation and inspiration.

- Feelings of confusion, uncertainty, and insecurity, which can make it difficult for them to make decisions or take action on their creative ideas.

- Feelings of overwhelmed by the number of options available, and may be unable to choose which direction to take their work in.

- Singer may find it hard to connect with their own emotions and convey them to the audience, resulting in a less impactful performance.

- Songwriters may find it hard to tap into their own emotional and experiences to create meaningful lyrics and music.

Additionally, singers and songwriters may experience a lack of confidence in their abilities, which can further impede their creative process. They may also struggle with feelings of self-doubt and insecurity, which can make it difficult for them to share their work with others or perform in front of an audience.

Being in a state of reversal may also cause feelings of fear, overwhelm, anxiety, or depression, which can negatively impact creativity and the ability to access positive emotions and inspiration.

Additionally, it may make it harder for a person to access their vocal range or to perform with confidence and expressiveness.

Resistance (Push/Pull): This is when your energy is blocked or hindered in some way. You are going in the right direction, but your desire is just out of reach. In the context of singing and songwriting, this could manifest in the following ways:

- Difficulty putting ideas or emotions into words or music

- Struggles with stage fright or performance anxiety

- Constantly feeling overwhelmed with information overload

- Difficulty collaborating with other musicians or industry professionals

- Resistance to change or trying new things in their music

- Difficulty accepting criticism or feedback

- A tendency to cling to a specific style or image, even if it no longer feels authentic or true to oneself.

"How could this affect Singers and Songwriters, if their energy is in resistance?"

- Resistance to the flow state can affect singers and songwriters by making it difficult for them to access their creative abilities and produce new music.

- They may struggle to find inspiration, and their writing may become forced or uninspired.

- Singers may have difficulty accessing the full range and power of their voice, which can affect the quality of their performances.

- It can also lead to frustration and mental block which could affect the overall output.

- Singers and songwriters may experience a lack of motivation or confidence in their abilities, which can further impede their creative process.

- They may also struggle with feelings of self-doubt and insecurity, which can make it difficult for them to share their work with others or perform in front of an audience.

- Resistance can also affect the emotional expression and interpretation of songs.

- Singer may find it hard to connect with their own emotions and convey them to the audience, resulting in a less impactful performance.

- Songwriters may find it hard to tap into their own emotional experiences to create meaningful lyrics.

To overcome this, singers and songwriters may need to take a break from their work, engage in activities that help them relax, utilise the techniques within this book to dissolve the energy reversals and energy resistances, or if nothing else is working, to seek professional help.

Flow (Aligned/Alignment): The concept of "energy flow" refers to a state in which one's energy is balanced and flowing freely, allowing them to fully express themselves and manifest their goals and desires easily. In the context of singing and songwriting, this could manifest in the following ways:

- A natural ability to express yourself through music and lyrics

- A strong connection to your emotions and the ability to convey them authentically in your music

- A steady stream of inspiration and creativity

- The ability to collaborate easily with other musicians and industry professionals

- A willingness to take risks and try new things in your music

- The ability to accept criticism and feedback as an opportunity for growth

- A sense of balance and harmony between your personal and professional lives.

All of these structures, states and systems in the physical body work together to maintain the body's energy balance and promote overall health. It's important to note that the body's energy system is also linked to the energetic body, which is an interconnected system of energy pathways that run through the physical body. These pathways, known as meridians in traditional Chinese medicine, connect the physical body to the body's energy centers, called chakras, which are linked to the body's emotional, mental, and spiritual well-being.

Using the different techniques shown within this book will enable you to dissolve any hidden blocks and balance within your energy, to allow you to be in Flow (aligned/alignment) state daily.

"If a Singer or Songwriter is in the flow state (energy aligned) how would they know?"

A person in a flow state may feel:

- Fully immersed and focused on their creative task, with a sense of effortless concentration, and enjoyment.

- May lose track of time and become unaware of their surroundings.

- A heightened sense of creativity, inspiration, self-awareness, clarity of thought, and a sense of inner satisfaction with their work.

- In sync with the task at hand, in control and operating at peak performance

- A sense of deep enjoyment and intrinsic motivation

- Like everything just comes to them naturally.

However, it's important to note that everyone's experience of flow state can be different, and some people may not experience all of these symptoms, or experience others.

Now you understand what energy alignment, energy bodies energy structures and which of the three states your energy flow can be in, we can now move onto what's hidden within your energy, and show you simple ways to identify it, and dissolve whatever is holding you back from accelerating your success in your indie singer and songwriting career, and life.

Keep on reading....

Testimonial

"I have suffered with overwhelm and anxiety for about 15 years, especially in my job. I was at the the end of my tether with managing it, but didn't want to be on medication. I never thought something this simple and affordable would help me but it did. I can not thank you enough."
Casey James, Songwriter, Massachusetts, USA

****

Remember to join the **FACEBOOK** group as it's a community and support systems, that will help you on your journey to consciousness, and accelerating your success with like-minded indie singers and songwriters, and my team. Share with us your revelations, your questions, your queries, and your breakthroughs: Accelerate Your Success Indie Music

Not on FB and have a question for me?
Ask by visiting www.beebyleighmusic.com.
I'd love to hear from you.

EXERCISE TWO

Create A Visual
"TIMELINE LIFE MAP"

This is a SUPER powerful exercise that will help you within future chapters to have a bird's eye view of your life and to see what you perceived as positive and negative along the way on a single trajectory. It can be a tool to make conscious self-directed changes that, literally, rewire your brain to heal itself. Known as plasticity, your brain has an innate capacity to make changes in positive, healing directions. Like other tools, you need to know it's there to access, and how to use it. The first step is to create the "Timeline Life Map", and then we can transform the energy attached to known and unknown events in both your past, present and future that are creating blocks in your energy.

Create your life-long timeline from birth all the way through to where you are now, and write down all of the milestones that you can think of, and they don't all have to be big ones like getting married. They could be little ones like, singing in the nativity play at age 5yrs, whatever it is. You will know they're milestones because they made you feel a certain way, either they made you feel great or they made you feel awful. Draw a line on a piece of paper or on the computer and section your line into years from birth to today and then add 6 month markers. Above the line put all positive milestones (what made you feel great), and below the line put all the negative milestones (what made you feel awful) in the relevant year and 6 month markers.

As you create each milestone, ask yourself these four questions and write down the answers for a future exercise:

- "What does someone experiencing this milestone believe about themselves?"
- "How has this milestone caused me to enter into stories that don't serve me now?"
- "Who or What am I blaming for where my life went from this milestone?"
- "What is it about my life and my experience up until this point that has caused me to think, believe or manifest these things or to take action in a certain way?"

I know it can be triggering, I know it can feel time consuming, but there are so many answers in your life experience to this point that are going to unlock the doors for success for you, so please do the work, create your timeline, ask the questions, journal on all of these things, as it will be well worth your time to help you accelerate your success.

Have a question for me?
Ask by visiting www.beebyleighmusic.com.
I'd love to hear from you.

CHAPTER THREE
Identifying Hidden Blocks

As an indie singer songwriter, myself, I spent years purchasing courses, joining groups, webinars, hiring marketing & social media experts, and mentors that promised they had the unique information and expertise that would help my singing and songwriting career skyrocket, and how to become wealthy doing what I loved full time.

These ranged from singing & songwriting lessons, branding gurus, business gurus, social media training, how to produce at home, and how to get more fans and the list goes on. Although many of them were very useful, the big thing that all these music & producing courses, academy training, business courses failed to talk about or address is the #1 reason people fail or struggle in their careers, or life. Which is that they have hidden blocks putting their energy out of alignment, and how to get it back into alignment to actually accelerate success that lasts.

I am sure many of the courses or training you have invested in yourself over the years, did not address this fundamental issue either. Yes; it may of touch on "mindset", but trying to fix only your mindset is like trying to push water uphill, and only plastering over the issue temporarily and not actually addressing the root cause.

Which is why releasing years of wired imprinting, programming, conditioning, trauma, beliefs, patterns and emotional set points that we have all pick up as children from generational, societal, religion and culture learnings is what this book will focus on helping you dissolve. I'll go into these topics in more depth later in the book; however, just know that leaving these negative beliefs, emotions, patterns, fears etc hidden in your energy and not realigning your energy to success, will be the main reason you remain on the struggling musician hamster wheel, going nowhere fast.

Singing and creating songs are some of the most creative and expressive activities that a person can engage in. When it comes to singers and songwriters, they offer a unique opportunity to share energy and emotions with others through music. These artists use their voices and words to share their stories, to express themselves and connect with others. And while doing so, many singers and songwriters often experience fear of the unknown, fear of vulnerability, fear of change, fear of success or failure, overwhelm, low vibrational beliefs about themselves, and the biggest challenges for many is the feelings of imposter syndrome, lack of trust, and the belief they are not, lovable or deserving enough – more on this in future chapters.

When you step into the power of your unique talents and gifts, fears may surface sometimes even seeming unrelated to your career, or to what you are currently doing at that moment in time. You may feel overwhelmed by the possibility of what could happen, and this could happen to you each time you launch a new song, promote yourself, have to go on stage or social media live, or tour. It is important to understand that these fears are based in duality and polarity. They are not real, but rather projections and illusions of what you believe could happen. By dissolving all blocks that keep you attached to these fears, you can align your energy and reframe your mindset to step into the power of your gifts with greater confidence. Creating powerful connections with others on a deeper level and like a magnet.

An Example: Since the pandemic the world has changed and so has the music industry. Whether you are new to the industry, or have been a part of it for years these major changes of how people promote their music, how they are visible to the world has become more technology based.

When the pandemic hit and lots of live shows and tours shut down, I had an increased number of clients coming to me with fears of having to do live performance over social media. As they had been so used to only using social media as a way to get their fans to turn up at their live shows, with posts and short videos, but now suddenly them and their bands were in separate houses and doing live shows.

Which meant appearing in little boxes on a screen all front and centre with no dark corners of the stage to hide for any of the musician, and the competition felt like it was growing out of control with everyone suddenly learning how to produce for themselves at home. What was once a hobby could be turned into a profitable business. Fears of IT issues, visibility, social media and more just caused an increase in fear and overwhelm.

In this section I will explain some of the common themes most of my client Indie Singers and Songwriters battle with in their energy, that they reflect into their reality:

"What Are Some Common Fears?"

Everyone on the planet suffers from fear, whether they are aware of it or not, and for those that live a life of anxiety, this is just part of the family of "fear" that has frozen in your energy keeping you in "Fight, Fright, Flight, and Freeze mode" continuously. Do you resonate to any of the below fears, or anxiety, if yes, I will show you how to easily and simply dissolve these and any others you may personally have in your energy (from the root), in future chapters!

- Fear of too much competition in the music industry. With more technologies / streaming services, the music industry has become increasingly competitive. This can be a daunting and an overwhelming prospect for many who are already struggling to make a name for themselves.

- Fear of not being good enough, loveable enough or deserving enough. Often creating self-doubt preventing many from reaching full potential and achieving success.

- Fear of rejection. It can be difficult to get your music heard by the right people. This fear can hold many back from sharing their music or being visible on social media, ultimately hindering their success.

- Fear of not being able to break through to the mainstream, or being overshadowed by more established artists.

- Fear of not being able to make a living off of music, or being taken seriously as an artist.

- Fear of not being able to release new music consistently, or be able to financially maintain their career

"What Is Imposter Syndrome?"

Imposter syndrome is the psychological condition of feeling that you are not worthy or deserving. Some of the common reasons many indie singers and songwriters clients suffer with Imposter Syndrome are:

- Feeling like they don't deserve the success they've achieved. Since many good singers and songwriters lack a degree or other credentials in the field of music; success has often come about instinctively. Without credentials, it's common to feel that you've come about your success without, as they say, "paying your dues". This fear of being exposed leads to feelings of self-doubt, insecurity and feeling unsafe.

- They are constantly comparing themselves to other artists, and they often feel like they don't measure up. They doubt their talent and ability, and this leads to a feeling of being an imposter.

- They feel like they're only pretending to be musicians. They worry that people will find out that they their success is just a fluke.

- This fear of being exposed can lead to a lot of judgement on themselves and projections onto others.

- They feel like they're not good enough, and that someone is going to catch on sooner or later. They worry that their fans or followers will eventually realise that they are a fraud, and this can be very debilitating.

Imposter syndrome can indirectly lead to stage or social media fright and writer's block, because most creative blocks come about as a result of a fear of failure. And since imposter syndrome means that you question the honesty of your efforts, you can start to fear that your next attempt at a song is going to fail, and soon everyone will know that you've simply been pretending.

The truth is: Great songs don't come about because you've got a degree, or because you know how to read and write music, or that you have any credentials at all. Great songs come from your life experiences, your heart energy, your talent, and knowing how to take listeners on a few minutes journey that pulls them in and connects to them on an emotional level.

If you've written or sung a song that you like, and that others like to listen to, you've done exactly what you're supposed to do. You're not an imposter: you're a singer-songwriter.

Common Reasons For Overwhelm & Burnout

- The new music industry is constantly changing, and it can be difficult to keep up with the latest trends and strategies. This makes it challenging to find success as an indie artist.

- There is a lot of competition out there, and it can be tough to stand out from the crowd. It's easy to feel discouraged when your music isn't getting the attention you hoped for.

- Often, you have to wear many hats, handling all aspects of you career yourself. This can be a lot of work, and it's easy to feel overwhelmed if things aren't going well.

- There's a lot of pressure to create new and innovative music, which can be daunting and lead to feelings of anxiety, which is just another word for "fear".

- *High workload and tight schedules*: The demands of touring, recording, writing, and promoting can be intense and create a high level of stress and workload.

- *Pressure to perform*: The pressure to consistently deliver high-quality performances and meet the expectations of fans and the industry can be a significant source of stress and burnout.

- *Creative block*: Difficulty with songwriting, vocal performance, or creative expression can lead to frustration and burnout.

- *Lack of self-care*: Neglecting self-care, such as adequate sleep, exercise, and healthy eating habits can contribute to burnout.

- *Financial stress*: The financial instability of the music industry, combined with the high cost of touring, recording and promoting, can create significant stress and burnout.

- **Personal issues:** Personal problems such as relationship issues, health concerns, or family problems can also contribute to burnout.

"What Are Common Signs Of Overwhelm?"

- **Decreased energy levels:** Overwhelm can cause physical and emotional exhaustion, reducing the energy levels required for creative expression and performance.

- **Stressed state of mind:** Chronic stress can disrupt the ability to focus and access the flow state necessary for creative expression.

- **Negative self-talk:** Overwhelm can lead to negative self-talk, decreased confidence, and a lack of belief in one's abilities.

- **Disconnection from source of inspiration:** Overwhelm can create a sense of disconnection from one's passions and sources of inspiration.

- **Reduced connection with audience:** Overwhelm can lead to decreased engagement with the audience and fans, reducing the connection and energy exchange during performance.

"What Are Common Signs Of Burnout?"

- **Loss of passion and motivation:** Burnout can lead to a loss of passion and motivation for music, reducing the energy and drive necessary for creative expression.

- **Decreased energy levels:** Burnout can cause physical and emotional exhaustion, making it difficult to maintain the energy levels required for performance.

- **Difficulty accessing inspiration:** Burnout can lead to a sense of disconnection from one's sources of inspiration, making it challenging to access the flow state necessary for creative expression.

- **Negative self-talk:** Burnout can lead to negative self-talk and decreased confidence in one's abilities, putting a singer or songwriter out of energetic alignment with their own talents and skills.

- **Reduced connection with audience:** Burnout can lead to decreased engagement with the audience and fans, reducing the connection and energy exchange during performance.

These overwhelm and burnout factors can significantly impact a singer or songwriter's ability to create and perform at their best, putting them out of energetic alignment with their art and audience.

Have a question for me?
Ask by visiting www.beebyleighmusic.com.
I'd love to hear from you.

CHAPTER FOUR
Lack, Scarcity and Poverty (Energy Blocks)

Lack, scarcity and poverty is deeply ingrained in many people's belief systems. This programming can come from our families, our cultures, or even the societies in which we live. It can be very difficult to break free of these limiting beliefs and allow money and wealth to flow freely in our lives without dissolving the blocks and limitations from our energies.

One of the main blocks to having abundance is the fear of not having enough. This fear can be caused by a variety of factors, including past experiences with money, or negative programming that tells us that we are not worthy of wealth and prosperity. When we hold on to these beliefs, it becomes very difficult for money and wealth to flow into our lives.

Another block to wealth consciousness is the belief that money is bad or evil. This belief often comes from a place of lack and scarcity, and is based on the idea that if we have money, we will become greedy and selfish. This is simply not true! When we dissolve this from our energy and shift our mindset, we begin to see money as a tool for creating positive change in the world, and opening ourselves up to infinite and limitless possibilities.

One way to begin to change our relationship with money is to start calling in surprise money. This means dissolving any blocks and beliefs that are preventing you from receiving financial abundance, and then asking the universe for help in manifesting more money into our lives through the power of quantum questions. The key is to stay open and receptive to the flow of wealth and abundance, and not put any limitations on what is possible, for miraculous results!

"What ways do Singers and Songwriters limit money flow with Lack, Scarcity, Poverty beliefs, patterns or blocks?"

- *Underestimating their worth:* Believing they don't deserve to be paid well for their work or that they are not valuable as artists can lead to accepting less than fair compensation.

- *Reluctance to invest:* The fear of failure or not succeeding can lead to a reluctance to invest in their careers or take calculated financial risks.

- **Limiting Beliefs**: Holding limiting beliefs about money, such as "money is hard to come by" or "you can't make a living as a musician," can prevent singers and songwriters from seeking out and taking advantage of financial opportunities.

- **Settling for less**: A lack of confidence in their abilities or a belief that opportunities are limited can lead to settling for lower paying gigs or less favourable contracts.

- **Not pursuing multiple streams of income**: Singers and songwriters may limit their earning potential by relying solely on performing and writing as sources of income, instead of exploring other revenue streams such as merchandise sales, streaming royalties, or licensing deals.

- **Avoiding marketing and promotion**: A belief that they are not worthy of success or that their work is not good enough can lead to a lack of marketing and promotion efforts, limiting their exposure and earning potential.

- **Overworking**: Overworking and not setting boundaries can lead to burnout and decreased productivity, reducing their earning potential and overall financial success.

What is the long term affects to a Singer and Songwriter if they have generational Lack, Scarcity and Poverty beliefs, patterns or blocks?

It may negatively impact their ability to be successful in the long term. These beliefs can lead to a lack of motivation, difficulty in taking risks and making decisions, and an inability

to see opportunities for growth and advancement. It may make it difficult for the individual to believe in their own talents and abilities, leading to self-doubt and a lack of confidence in their own work. This can make it difficult for them to market themselves and their music effectively, which can limit their potential for success. This can also lead to a lack of financial stability and security, which can make it difficult for the individual to sustain a career in the music industry.

They may also struggle with feelings of inadequacy, self-doubt, and comparison with others in the industry, which lead to limiting oneself and not putting oneself out there. This can make it difficult for them to build a loyal fan base and gain recognition in the industry. This can affect the emotional and mental well-being of the individual, leading to anxiety, depression, and other mental health issues. This can make it difficult for them to focus on their work, maintain healthy relationships, and make sound decisions. Overall, beliefs, mindset, and energetic blocks of lack, scarcity, and poverty can have a detrimental impact on a singer or songwriter's career and personal life, and it is important for them to work on dissolving and changing these beliefs in order to achieve long-term success.

It's important to note that having a lack, scarcity, or poverty mindset is not a character flaw or a permanent state, and it is possible to dissolve and change these beliefs and patterns within your energy using the techniques shown within this book.

"How would a Singer or Songwriter know if they have Lack, Scarcity, or Poverty mindset, beliefs, patterns or blocks?"

- Constant thoughts of not having enough, whether it be time, money, resources, or talent

- Difficulty in setting and achieving goals, or feeling like success is unattainable

- Difficulty in taking risks and trying new things, due to fear of failure or lack of resources

- Difficulty in seeing opportunities for growth and advancement, or building a loyal fan base due to a belief that they are not worthy or capable.

- Difficulty in believing in their own talents and abilities, leading to self-doubt and a lack of confidence in their own work

- Difficulty in valuing their own work and pricing it appropriately

- Difficulty in accepting compliments and positive feedback, or feeling like it's not deserved

"What's are typical behaviours or Actions of Singers or Songwriters with Lack, Scarcity or Poverty beliefs, blocks, patterns or mindset?"

- Constantly comparing oneself to others in the industry and feeling inadequate

- Having difficulty in asking for help or support from others

- Being overly critical of oneself and others

- Being overly focused on the negative aspects of one's life and career

- Having difficulty in accepting and spending money

- Having difficulty in making decisions

- Being pessimistic about the future

- Being overly cautious and avoiding taking risks

- Being overly self-sacrificing, taking on too many responsibilities, and neglecting self-care

It's important to keep in mind that having some of these thoughts or behaviours doesn't necessarily mean that someone has a poverty, scarcity or lack mindset, but when it becomes a pattern and affects one's life, career and well-being it's important to check that these are not hidden or frozen within your energy causing blocks.

You can check with the technique I am about to show you, called "The Sway" technique which is based around Kinesiology to what you have in your energy that needs to be dissolved / removed.

One of the most common questions I get asked is:

> *"Beeby, What if I don't know what is hidden in my energy, how do I know what to dissolve and from where in my energy it needs to be dissolved?"*

Don't worry, I've got you covered, keep on reading….

****

Remember to join the **FACEBOOK** group as it's a community and support systems, that will help you on your journey to consciousness, and accelerating your success with like-minded indie singers and songwriters and my team. Share with us your revelations, your questions, your queries, and your breakthroughs: Accelerate Your Success Indie Music

Not on FB and have a question for me?
Ask by visiting www.beebyleighmusic.com.
I'd love to hear from you.

EXERCISE THREE

Identify What's In Your Energy With The "THE SWAY TECHNIQUE"

It is recommended to perform the "Sway Technique" in a quiet and undisturbed environment, avoiding any distractions.

For the purpose of this example, we are going to use the emotion of **FEAR** to test if you have fear in your energy.

However, once you have learnt the steps to this technique, you will be able to replace this with any question you wish to ask your energy, as long as it's a question that can provide a YES / NO answer, as otherwise the sway technique will not work.

Step 1:
- I invite you to stand with your feet hip width apart, or if you are unable to stand feel free to sit on the edge of a chair.

- I want you to close your eyes and relax (take some deep breaths to relax if needed).

- I want you to repeat this question out loud **"Am I carrying feelings of FEAR in my energy?"**

Step 2:

- Your body is going to respond and give you an answer, as what you are accessing here is information held in your subconscious and Akashic records.

- Usually a movement or sway forward will be a "YES" and, usually a movement or sway backwards will be a "NO"

- This sensation maybe very subtle or gentle to start with, this is definitely something to practice as by practicing, your sway will get bigger and more obvious to the answer that you are being given.

Step 3:

- Using the sway technique in step one, ask this question. "Do I have resistance and/or energy reversals that would stop me from dissolving this **FEAR** from my energy today?"

- If you get a "NO' proceed to step 4, if you get a "Yes" release the energy reversals and/or resistance first by saying out loud once.

- "I am ready to release all and any resistance and/or reversals that are stopping me from dissolving **"FEAR"** from my energy today", I dissolve this from both my energy, and my reflections into my reality. In all forms, on all levels, and throughout time, consciousness and beyond."

- Ask the question again from step 1 and if you get a "YES" again just repeat the release statement from step 3 once more, before moving onto step 4.

Step 4:

- This is where you get to transform the energy, dissolve it and let it go from all energy fields, before moving to step 5 where you will align your energy and reprogram it.

- You will need to say the statement out loud three times, and take a deep breath between each of the three times that you say the statement out loud.

- "I am ready to dissolve all **FEAR** that is hidden, attached or frozen anywhere or everywhere within my energy. I dissolve this from both my energy, and my reflections into my reality. In all forms, on all levels, and throughout time, consciousness and beyond."

Step 5:

- This is where you get to align your energy and reprogram it with a technique called "Future Forward Manifesting."

"FUTURE FORWARD MANIFESTING"

Once you have done all four steps, use this "Future Forward Manifesting" technique to allow your subconscious and energy to catch up with your desires.

On the next page you will see a few example questions related to singers and songwriters, but feel free to change the wording to align to your career and life desires. It can be changed to anything, as long as it is worded positively, and the question is worded as if you have already received it.

For step 5, you only need to pick one or two questions each time to say out loud, three times. At the end of each sentence say **"Thank you, and so it is done"**

- "I am so grateful for the sold-out shows and the overwhelming response from my fans."

- "I am so grateful for my amazing team of industry professionals who support and guide me in my career."

- "I am so grateful for the recognition and accolades I have received in the industry."

- "I am so grateful for the abundance and financial success that my music career brings me."

- "I am so grateful for my constant flow of creative inspiration and the ability to write hit songs."

- "I am so grateful for my strong personal brand and the ability to stand out in the industry."

- "I am so grateful for the abundance of opportunities that come my way to showcase my music."

- "I am so grateful for my positive mindset, self-confidence and the motivation to keep going in my career."

These affirmations are written in a "present tense" as if you've already received, as this helps your subconscious mind and energy to believe that these things are already **true** and in turn aligns your thoughts, emotions and actions to manifest your desires in a more speedy and effortless way.

You can now use "The Sway Technique" to remove any themes that you became conscious of when doing the *"Timeline Life Map"* in exercise two (2), which was at the end of chapter two (2).

Testimonial

Beeby supported me through some tough times and helped me feel that I had worth. She is awesome, supportive. non judgmental. Genuinely wants the best for her clients. Thank you Beeby. You made a massive difference for me.
Ella McCready, Singer-Songwriter, UK

****

Remember to join the **FACEBOOK** group as it's a community and support systems, that will help you on your journey to consciousness, and accelerating your success with like-minded indie singers and songwriters and my team. Share with us your revelations, your questions, your queries, and your breakthroughs: <u>Accelerate Your Success Indie Music</u>

Not on FB and have a question for me?
Ask by visiting <u>www.beebyleighmusic.com</u>.
I'd love to hear from you.

CHAPTER FIVE
Disempowering Relationships

Most of us without realising are out of alignment "out of flow" in our energy due to the relationship connections we have in our lives. As the majority of people are still living in the old paradigm way, where we have been programmed to be in one of three energetic states "shown on the Karpman drama triangle diagram" on the next page. The pusher (Persecutor), the puller (Victim) or protector (Rescuer). We interchange roles depending on the scenario, person, and/or experience. This could be several times a day.

To understand this further; most of us have grown up watching TV series, and/or films that liken to this Karpman drama triangle with scripts having a "good character", "bad character" and the character that needs "rescuing". As all three of these states are disempowering to our energy, it makes us out of alignment on a daily, or regular basis.

The Drama Triangle
Old Paradigm Way Of Living

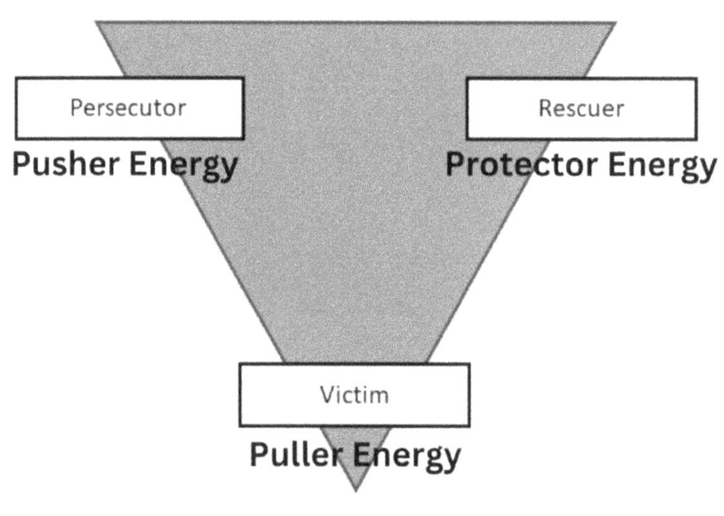

Victim/Puller (Needs Rescuing): This is the state where someone is reaching out for support, not ready to heal. Stuck in a continuous loop of stories and drama within the experience or relationship, having negative beliefs, and fighting to not take blame, responsibility or be at fault within the experience, situation or relationship.

We've all been in this state, as it's the state of needing "love and validation". We learn as babies that if we cry someone comes to rescue us, and we continue this pattern through our lives, not realising that it is disempowering and taking us out of alignment.

Persecutor/Pusher (Bad Character): This is the state where someone is pushing or projecting their energy, opinions on you, and they think it is ok to tell you what they think of you without being asked. They forcefully direct their anger, energy and attention at you, and expect you to take it. They never take responsibility for themselves, and will redirect whatever is going on in their life back at you.

Rescuer/Protector (Good Character): This is the state where people end up, when they grow out of victim mode. As most of us want to feel like "we are doing our best by people", looking after, supporting and being there for others. However, often this is at the detriment and better judgement of ourselves. You will know you are in this state when you do something for somebody, and then you are really annoyed when they don't say "Thank you or give you recognition". You'll likely turn to a friend with a list of all the things you've done for that other person, with no payoff.

It is important to note that very often we are playing out all three energetic states (three character roles) within our own energy, when it comes to the relationship with ourselves. Which constantly takes us out of alignment as we contradict ourselves internally.

Through the techniques in this book, you will learn how to be conscious of what state you are in, and how to move to being "In Your Power" from a place of LOVE (the centre position of the triangle).

"What is Gaslighting and how does it affect Singers and Songwriters, and Relationships?"

Gaslighting has become a bit of a buzz word over the past few years, and many of us believe that we've never been impacted with this behaviour, so tend to dismiss delving into what it is really about. I hadn't planned to include this section within this book, however after working with a high percentage of clients that had gaslighting energies attached to them, or energy blocks connected to gaslighting, I decided that this section could be extremely valuable to you. Left in your energy it could have a major impact on all your relationships within your life, including the relationship with yourself.

Gaslighting in the music industry refers to manipulative and psychological tactics used by individuals or groups to control and exploit musicians, particularly in the context of power dynamics and control over their careers. This can include denying the validity of their experiences, manipulating information, denying promises made, and making them question their own memory and perception of events.

This can also be manipulation of an individual's perception of their own voice, lyrics, or songwriting abilities. This can include denying the validity of their own creative vision, making them question their own talent, and attempting to control the way they express themselves artistically. Both these type of manipulation can occur between artists, producers, and industry executives, to name just a few, leading to harm and a suppression of creative expression, and harm and exploitation within your career with the music industry.

Please be aware though that gaslighting is not solely connected to the music industry or other artists, gaslighting can happen in any industry, or by any person that you spend time with in your personal life too.

"How would a Singer or Songwriter know they are being Gaslighted?"

- *Doubt in their own abilities*: They begin to question their own voice, lyrics, or songwriting skills, even though they previously felt confident in them.

- *Inaccurate feedback*: They receive feedback that contradicts what they know to be true about their own abilities.

- *Isolation*: They are deliberately isolated from their support network, making it harder for them to get validation and affirmation from others.

- *Control over their creative vision:* They feel like someone else is controlling their creative vision and making decisions for them, rather than allowing them to have agency over their own art.

- *Manipulative behaviour:* They feel like someone is deliberately manipulating their perceptions, experiences, and memories to make them doubt themselves.

If someone is experiencing these types of behaviours, the two step approach would be to use the techniques in this book to dissolve everything within your energy, to ensure you are not mirroring this out into your reality for more experiences similar, and to also reach out for help and support from trusted friends, family, or professionals.

"What are subtle ways Singers / Songwriters get Gaslighted without realising?"

- Being told they're "too sensitive" or "overreacting" when they express concerns.

- Constant critique and criticism of their work, leading to self-doubt and insecurity.

- Being subjected to lies and contradictory statements, causing them to doubt their own sanity.

- Being made to feel responsible for problems that aren't their fault.

- Having their accomplishments and achievements minimised or dismissed.

- Being manipulated into thinking their own memories are inaccurate.

- Being gaslighted by someone they trust and care about, making it difficult to recognise the behaviour as abusive.

- Having their perceptions and beliefs constantly questioned, leading to confusion and uncertainty.

- Being made to feel isolated and alone, with no one to turn to for support.

"How do Singers and Songwriters Gaslight themselves?"

We don't just get gaslighted by others, the majority of us gaslight ourselves without even realising it. However, this behaviour causes us to be taken completely out of alignment within our energy.

Gaslighting oneself would involve denying one's own experiences, talent, or worth as a creative person. This could manifest in various ways, such as denying the impact of one's own work, minimising one's achievements, or disregarding one's own instincts and creativity. Such self-doubt, self-criticism can lead to negative consequences for the artist and their work, and it's important for creative individuals to cultivate self-awareness and self-compassion.

"What is the long term affects on a Singer or Songwriter that is holding trauma of Gaslighting themselves or being gaslighted by others within their energy?"

Gaslighting can have long-term negative effects on a person's mental health, including anxiety, depression, low self-esteem, and a lack of trust in oneself and others. This can also affect their creativity and ability to perform as a singer or songwriter. It's important for individuals to seek support and help in overcoming such trauma, and to focus on self-care and building resilience. By using any one of the techniques explained within this book, you can completely dissolve and remove all past gaslighting effects that may have been frozen, attached or hidden within your energy.

"What are Energy Drains (Energy Vampires)?"

Energy drains (or as I like to call them Energy Vampires), are negative things, people or environments that can pull our energy down and prevent us from achieving success. Things like stress, fears, negative relationships or people who are negative and drain our energy with their words or actions.

I'm sure we've all experienced people in our lives that are "glass half empty", "critical" or project "lack mentality", or you may have been in environments that are too noisy, cluttered or unhygienic that immediately drain our energies from just being there. If you've ever walked into a room and felt metaphorically like you could "cut the atmosphere with a knife", then you have experienced an energy draining environment.

What most people are unaware of is that energy drains can attach themselves to our energy, and remain a block in our energy until identified and dissolved. This can sometimes cause us to act or respond in a way more suited to their energy, or identity than our own. It's important to be aware of these drains and do what we can to minimise their impact on your life and energy.

"What are some of the energy draining behaviours, and or environments for Singers and Songwriters?"

- Working with people who are unprofessional or unreliable.

- Being in a negative and toxic work environment.

- Performing in front of unappreciative or hostile audiences.

- Constantly dealing with rejection and criticism.

- Facing financial difficulties or insecurity.

- Having to deal with intense competition and pressure.

- Coping with chronic stress and burnout.

- Having to deal with constant negativity and drama from others.

- Dealing with creative blocks and lack of inspiration.

- Facing excessive demands and expectations from others.

"What are some of the Long term affects on a Singer or Songwriter experiencing energy draining behaviours, and or environments?"

- Burnout and loss of passion for music.

- Depression and anxiety (increased fears).

- Decreased creativity and productivity.

- Decreased self-esteem and confidence.

- Physical and mental exhaustion.

- Increased substance abuse or unhealthy coping mechanisms such as over eating.

- Deterioration in personal and professional relationships.

- Decreased ability to perform at their best.

- Stagnation or decline in career advancement.

- Chronic health problems such as stress-related illnesses.

By using any one of the techniques explained within this book, you can completely dissolve and remove all past or current drama triangles, gaslighting and or energy drains that may have be frozen or hidden within your energy.

EXERCISE FOUR

Identify What Areas Of Your Life Have Hidden Blocks "THE SWAY TECHNIQUE"

By using "The Sway Technique" shown in exercise three (3) at the end of chapter four (4). Sway on each of these life areas to see where you have hidden blocks that need to be investigated further. Once you have a (YES) or (NO) sway for each listed below, write it down, and I will show you how to dissolve these blocks "simply" in a future chapter with additional techniques.

Alternatively, you can use the Sway Technique shown in exercise three (3) to ask more questions around each life areas, and release the energy using the five (5) steps.

- Thoughts
- Emotions
- Physical Health
- Environment
- Relationships
- Lifestyle
- Money
- Passion & Purpose
- Making An Impact

CHAPTER SIX
Becoming Consciously Aware

One of the biggest secrets to life that I've learned is the necessity of making the unconscious conscious, the implicit into the explicit.

You are, right now, in this moment, already perfectly masterfully creating your life. You don't need any courses on manifestation. You are always perfectly, flawlessly manifesting your life.

The issue is that you've been doing it largely unconsciously. You've been unknowingly, unconsciously creating and literally forming your life out of the plethora of implicit beliefs, assumptions, rules, values and paradigms (Spells) that you are semi-consciously or unconsciously living.

My mission with this book is to give you the techniques to be able to go from unconsciously creating struggles to consciously creating your own success story, and expanding that out through your family and through your work, and through your whole life.

Imagine that this, not all of the conditioning you took on as a child, is your true identity. In this book, I will show you how to focus your awareness in such a way that you intentionally aim and channel all of that knowledge, information, wisdom, and power into the intentional conscious creation of everything that you want to make the success, health, wealth, relationships, life of your dreams.

As we go deeper, I will also show you how to dissolve, dismantle, and demolish all of the things that you have thus far created and manifested, as you unintentionally, unknowingly lived out all of your implicit (programmed) assumptions, beliefs, rules, values, and old paradigms.

Other Concepts

We'll also look at some other key concepts that will help your mind believe and understand, so that it can willingly join and support you as you begin to live what you know is true. We're going to help your mind through that process. (This is a very crucial missing key in much of the more "spiritually-advanced" personal development work available. If you've ever encountered a powerful, "obvious" spiritual truth and then felt unable to really be able to integrate it into your life, this missing element was probably partially at play.)

A lot of self-help approaches only work with the mind, and a lot of spiritual approaches try to go in direct opposition to the mind, but neither of those ways are sustainable, and neither really works. Another big myth out there is that meditation and "mind quieting" can do what's needed to make your ideal life happen. Perhaps they can help, to a certain extent, but the odds are high that you have felt bad about yourself for not being able to meditate or quiet your mind enough. Or maybe you have been able to meditate for years, but you're not seeing any changes in the deepest pain-spots of your life. We're going to dissolve all of that.

We're also going to look at the concept of "spells." I've referred to this concept already, but what is a spell? No doubt you are probably associating spells with something like, witches, cures or Halloween. The spells I am referring to are not related to any of those, but are very real in your energy.

You'll be surprised to learn that you have put yourself under hundreds, if not thousands, of them. As a child, you allowed family, society, education, the medical system, governmental systems, religious systems to place you under tens of thousands of spells. You're going to understand what they are, and how they work. You're also going to get access to more simple yet highly affective techniques to dissolve them.

We're also going to look at the "Theory of Constraints", which is one of the most radically powerful business concepts formulated. It is outrageously complex, yet can be distilled into a simple idea that you can apply to any part of your life to experience quantum leaps in consciousness, ability, and freedom in a matter of seconds.

We're also going to talk about paradigms and the levels of transformation that are available to you. We'll take a closer look at how you got to where you are, and how you can move out of it. We're going to look at how doing a "core paradigm shift" is the key missing ingredient in almost all approaches to personal development and self-help.

> *"Beeby, I'm afraid that I might have a fear of success? Is there such a thing, or is it all just fear of failure?"*

It's only fear. It's all the same fear." We're going to talk deeply about emotions, what they are and why they matter.

We're going to talk about how to become a conscious master of your emotions, directing your emotions to actually serve you, as well as following your emotions into more and more of the miracles you truly want to live in.

For now, I just want to acknowledge the reality that fear often comes up when a person begins to actually take steps into a life of miracles or even a life that "works".

You've probably heard about the amygdala, which is a part of the brain that some refer to as the "lizard brain" or the ancient, ancestral brain that is there to keep you safe. Your mind, particularly this old part of your mind, is not designed to be the driver of your life.

The mind is designed to be the navigator, but through our programming, through our training as children in our modern cultures, we've been taught to actually "let go of the wheel" on many topics. And when you release the wheel, the mind automatically grabs it and begins to drive.

Yet when the mind is driving, it really only understands one job, and that is to keep you safe. The only way that it knows how to do that, is to keep everything exactly the way that it is. In effect, it jerks the wheel to "lock" a hard left and keeps it there. (This is why you may eventually begin to notice that you are going in circles—that the landscape is beginning to be strangely familiar in your life or career…)

When we get ready to make a change, we immediately come face to face with all of the things that we ever placed between ourselves and that change, which includes all of our fears. This is normal. However, normal is rarely beneficial.

So, let's do something now to help make this change you're going through easier and smoother.

EXCERISE FIVE
"IDENTIFY FEAR"

Please write down a short paragraph in answer to this question: *"What do I fear might happen if I were to dare believe and actually step towards the life I want. To dare to take action towards it?"* Take a few minutes with this question and then answer as honestly as you possibly can.

To jog your thoughts (although your own answer will be the most helpful to you), here's an example: "I'm afraid I might fail, and I might find out that this book or system is another one that is all BS. I'm afraid I might lose friends or family if I up-level. I'm afraid I will grow but my partner won't, and I'll end up losing them or having to leave them or, worse, having to stay with them and pretend." etc.

As you continue to go through this book, I'll show you exactly how to dissolve your fears and obstacles, including the ones you just wrote down, so that you can be in a state of ever-present power and certainty, where moment by moment, you're creating more and more of the life you really want.

One of my clients, Karen, was suffering from severe fear of "putting herself out there". She's a brilliant singing with a lot to offer. She had wanted to start putting her songs into YouTube & TikTok videos to share with her audience. However, she was paralysed by fear. After a one to one session where we did a dissolving technique on her energy. Karen found the courage to show up and start posting her videos. She emailed afterwards to say that the knot in her stomach that had been there for 30 years was GONE. It dissolved during our short session. A year later, it is still gone.

> *"We only see what we want to see; we only hear what we want to hear. Our belief system is just like a mirror that only shows us what we believe."*
> **—Unknown**

Remember to join the FACEBOOK group as it's a community and support systems, that will help you on your journey to consciousness, and accelerating your success with like-minded indie singers and songwriters, and my team. Share with us your revelations, your questions, your queries, and your breakthroughs: Accelerate Your Success Indie Music

Not on FB and have a question for me?
Ask by visiting www.beebyleighmusic.com.
I'd love to hear from you.

EXCERISE SIX

Identify Hidden Blocks "MUSIC SOUL JOURNALING" TECHNIQUE

Music Soul Journaling, can help you to go deeper to intuitively uncover, discover, unhide, unfreeze what has been suppressed, hidden, frozen or stuck in your energy over time. This simple yet phenomenally effective technique can help you dissolve anything in your energy that does not serve you, simply by listening to two songs, and following the step by step guide.

GET STARTED

Find a quiet place where you will not be disturbed for @15-20 mins the maximum time required for part one and two.

To get started you will need a pen, journal (paper), tissues in case you get emotional and a drink to hand, preferably water for hydration.

Using headphones has a greater impact on the results; however they are not essential. Remember this is about your energy and subconscious and not what you think and feel about the song.

Music Soul Journaling
SONG 1

When you are ready go to any platform that you would usually listen to music on - for example: Spotify, Amazon, iTunes, Apple, YouTube etc…

Please note: **DO NOT** go to any playlists or songs that you have personally created on these platforms.

- Go to the homepage on your selected platform and then click on search bar.

- In the search bar type in: **"Emotional Playlists"** and then click on whatever playlist appears at the **very top** of that search.

It is important that you click the very top playlist, even if it's not a genre that you would usually listen to.

- Once you have selected that playlist

- Click on the song that is **7th** down from the very top (don't press play just yet).

Again, it is important that you click the **7th** down from the top song, even if it's not a genre or style of song that you would usually listen to.

- Set the intention that you are going to allow your subconscious mind to be open and curious, taking note of everything that comes to mind while listening.

It is important to journal after listening, and not during your listening time to enable you to be full present.

After listening to the song, you will need to write down everything that came to mind during that time, any thoughts, feelings, emotions, beliefs, any events, any people, any places, any visualisations that sprung to mind or resonated

Even if you think what came to mind was insignificant or unrelated to this exercise, subconsciously it maybe linked to something very significant within your energy that you need to dissolve. So write it down….

- Now it's time to put on your headphones (if available), and press play on your selected song.

- Close your eyes and listen to the music and lyrics if the song has any, allowing yourself to be open, curious and relaxed.

- Once the song has has finished press pause

- Write down anything that has come to mind while listening to this song – nothing is insignificant whether good or bad.

- If nothing came to mind yet you had sensations within your body, write down where they were happening, and what type of sensation it was e.g. cramp, pain, numbness etc.

Take as much time as you need before continuing

Emotional Scale

Once you have finished writing, look at what you have written and match overall how you are feeling post listening to the song.

The emotional scale may help you to identify the overall emotion you are feeling – you maybe feeling more than just one word. Write them all down on your journal too!

Now Go To ACTION Mantra One Statement

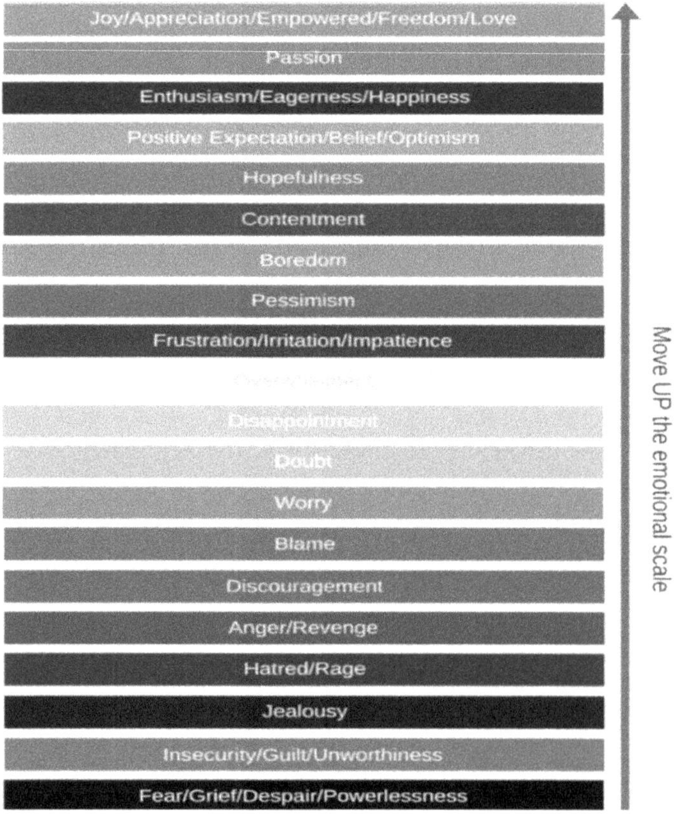

ACTION MANTRA ONE (1)
STATEMENT

Place your **LEFT HAND** on the journal (or paper) you have written on

With your **RIGHT HAND** tap with **index finger and middle finger** on your **HEART** as you say each word out loud to MANTRA ONE on the next page.

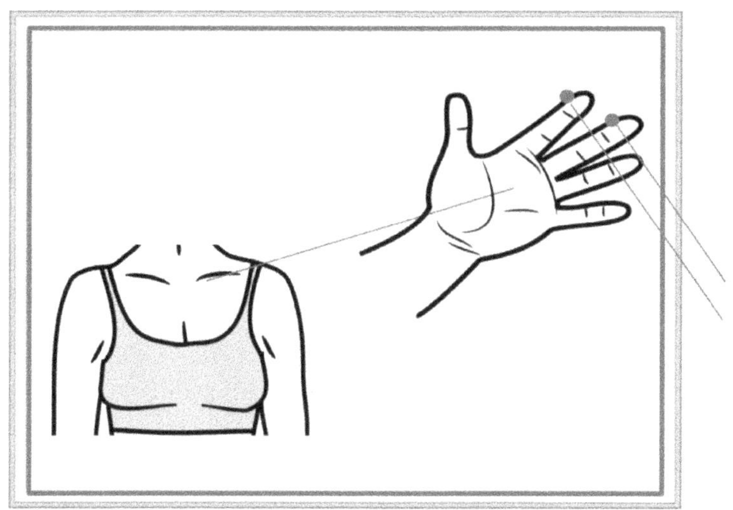

ACTION MANTRA ONE STATEMENT

- "Why am I no longer protecting my wounds and the trauma that has hidden, frozen or attached to my energy?". "Why have I dissolved, released and let go of all of this today?"
- "Why am I no longer triggered by my soul story?"
- "Why am I no longer carrying the shame that I associate with it?"
- "Why have I allowed myself to align to my high power and the power of love, to guide me, and do for me what I can not do for myself?"
- "Why have I allowed myself to be grounded, and my soul story and energy cleansed, for me to redesign my reality to the vision that I desire?"
- "Every moment of my life is an opportunity to choose to see through the lens of love and not through the lens of fear"
- "I have the power to love, I have the power to forgive, I have the power to succeed, and I have the power to be grateful"
- "To allow abundance to flow easily, consistently, and in large amounts. I am allowing myself to be free and finally safe"
- "I give my energy acceptance and authorisation to dissolve everything that I have journaled today. I let it go in: 7,6,5,4,3,2 and 1".
- Thank you and so it is done!!

Music Soul Journaling
SONG 2

Now you are going to repeat the steps from song one, but with a change to the playlist and song.

Remember: **DO NOT** go to any playlists or songs that you have personally created on these platforms.

- Go back to the homepage on your selected platform and then click on the search bar again.

- In the search bar type in: **"Freedom Playlists"** and then click on whatever playlist appears at the **very top** of that search.

It is important that you click the very top playlist, even if it's not a genre that you would usually listen to.

- Once you have selected that playlist

- Click on the song that is **7th** down from the very top (don't press play just yet).

Again, it is important that you click the **7th** down from the top song, even if it's not a genre or style of song that you would usually listen to.

- Set the intention that you are going to allow your subconscious mind to be open and curious, taking note of everything that comes to mind while listening.

It is important to journal after listening, and not during your listening time to enable you to be full present.

After listening to song two, you will need to write down everything that came to mind during that time, any thoughts, feelings, emotions, beliefs, any events, any people, any places, any visualisations that sprung to mind or resonated

Even if you think what came to mind was insignificant or unrelated to this exercise, subconsciously it maybe linked to something very significant within your energy that you need to dissolve. So write it down….

- Now it's time to put on your headphones (if available) again, and press play on your selected song.

- Close your eyes and listen to the music and lyrics if the song has any, allowing yourself to be open, curious and relaxed.

- Once the song has has finished press pause

- Write down anything that has come to mind while listening to this song – nothing is insignificant whether good or bad.

- If nothing came to mind yet you had sensations within your body, write down where they were happening, and what type of sensation it was e.g. cramp, pain, numbness etc.

Take as much time as you need before continuing

Emotional Scale

Again, once you have finished writing, look at what you have written and match overall how you are feeling post listening to the song.

The emotional scale may help you to identify the overall emotion you are feeling – you maybe feeling more than just one word. Write them all down on your journal too!

Now Go To ACTION Mantra Two Statement

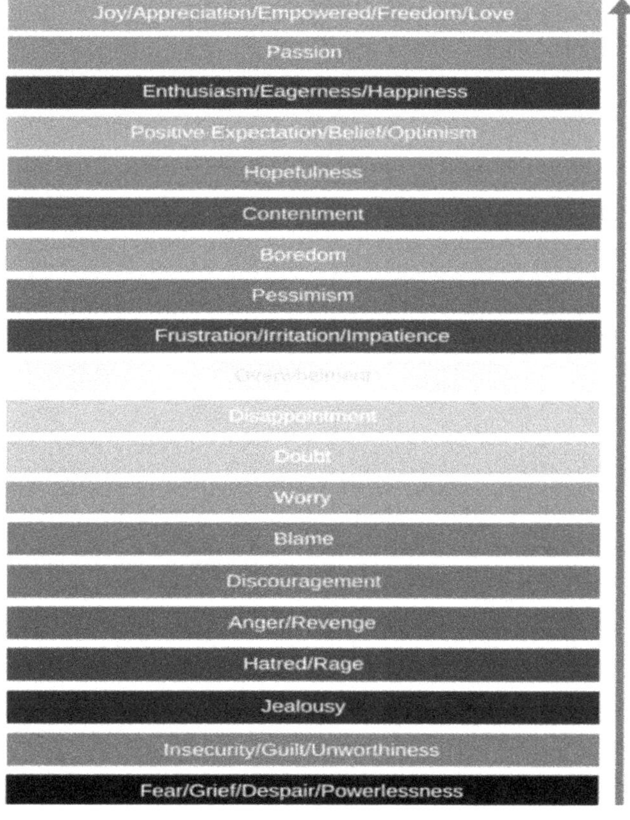

ACTION MANTRA TWO (2)
STATEMENT

Place your **LEFT HAND** on the journal (or paper) you have written on

With your **RIGHT HAND** tap with **index finger and middle finger** on your **HEART** as you say each word out loud to MANTRA ONE on the next page.

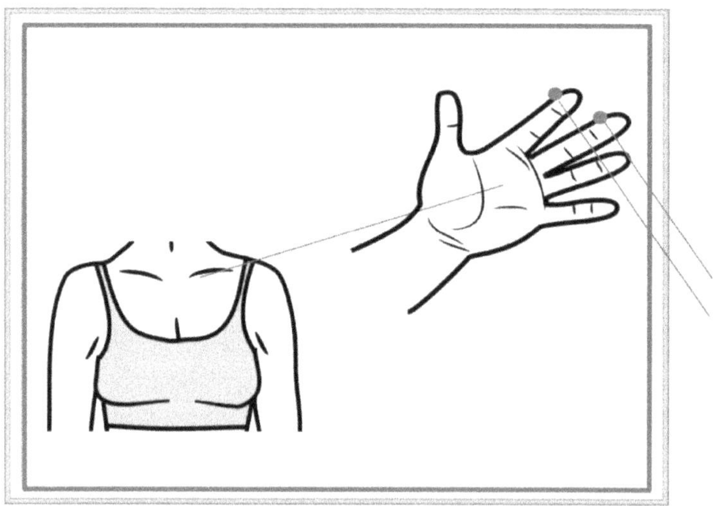

ACTION MANTRA TWO (2) STATEMENT

- "I give my acceptance and authorisation to allow into my energy, my mind, my heart, my body, and my soul story today, every positive pattern, every positive habit, every positive belief, every positive thought, every positive emotion, and all and any generational patterns that are for my highest good and my highest purpose"

- "I am allowing myself to be excepting of me, and allow connection to the power of love"

- "I am allowing all of the positivity's to radiate throughout my energy, my heart, and my soul story today"

- "I am allowing myself to be centred, grounded, happy, healthy and in flow. I am truly loved. I am allowing my soul story to shine"

- "I shine my light out into the world. As miracles happen in the light, and I chose to be seen in the light today"

- "I am allowing myself to let go of all that no longer serves me that I have journaled today".

- Why am I So Successful, So Abundant, So Truly Loved?" Why am I now Safe to be ME, and finally finally FREE?"

- "I allow all of this into my energy, my mind, my body, my heart and soul story today in: 7,6,5,4,3,2 and 1". Thank you and so it is done!!

"CONGRATULATIONS"

You Have Completed

MUSIC SOUL JOURNALING

POST FINISHING

As you will have only dissolved-released what you journaled today, along with all of the affects that are associated or attached to it. You can use Music Soul Journaling again and again to uncover what is hidden, frozen or stuck in your energy, that is no longer serving you.

Depending on the number of years you have held these things in your energy, will determine how long it will take to completely release from your energy. It is usually immediately or up to 7 days from completing all steps of the process.

SELF CARE

Stay hydrated and get plenty of rest. In some people; energy can release in a number of different ways from tiredness, cold like symptoms, burping, passing wind, yawning or in some very rare cases vomiting or diarrhoea. These are normal side effects in some people and it just means that the negative energy has dissolved and you are in the healing phase. Do not be alarmed if you have these symptoms or you if you do not, as everyone is different. However if these symptoms persist or are severe then contact your doctor.

CHAPTER SEVEN
"Spells" Keeping You Stuck

I've mentioned "spells" a few times already, and it is time to fully address the idea.

I offer the radical proposition that, behind it all, "spells" are the cause of pain, frustration, sadness, procrastination, fear, difficulty, feeling overwhelmed, depression, body issues, negative emotions, and all business, money and success limitations.

I know, I know, it sounds CRAZY and I thought exactly the same. So let me give you the evidence. For YOU to decide.

The Reality of Spells

Throughout history, select people have held the knowledge of the reality of spells. In recent times, science and religion have largely altered or erased knowledge of them.

For the majority of us, our only exposure to them today is through the "humorously superficial" form of cartoons or animated movies. The gravity and reality of spells has been relegated to silliness and or superstition.

In truth, spells are neither magical nor make-believe. And once you understand their inherent cost, they are definitely not silly.

A spell is a mental, emotional, and/or psychological state where one's behaviour is quite literally dictated to them, on one or more topics or areas of life by unconscious drivers. When activated, the person appears to have no ability to overcome their reactions to certain triggers.

Think, "Snow White". When the trigger flipped, she went to sleep, and she was frozen in that state, unable to move, until she was set free by a kiss of love.

You might be surprised to find how "true" that scenario is. For you. For everybody else. And on soooooooo many topics…

If heights don't bother you, then think about someone you know who is absolutely terrified of heights. They are under a spell that says, "heights are terrifying". It creates limiting behaviours and irrational reactions, and they are unable to see the roots of it.

Or someone who is terrified of singing live. They are trapped in the "singing live is terrifying" spell. It creates limiting behaviours and irrational actions that they can neither see nor alter.

Or think about someone who, no matter what they do, they just can't make money. They have all the skills and knowledge, talent and awareness, the information like everyone else, yet they just can't seem to make any money. They are under some form of, "money is hard" spell. Again, limiting behaviours and irrational actions follow. And they are unable to see or alter them. The list is endless.

"Is there an area of your life that you feel under a spell?"

Is there an area in which you seem to get irrationally afraid, angry, upset, or ineffective?

Have you tried to change some aspect of your life again and again, but it just doesn't change?

As I'll illustrate in just a moment, these painful areas of life are the result of a litany of spells. The Endless Loop of Spells

We have all these spells on specific topics. They are closely related to beliefs. They run as "topic-sensitive" programs in our energy system.

They cluster into groups of spells called "rules" and "values". These run as full-scale programs in our energy systems, and then the clusters group at a higher level into paradigms. They make up "everything we know" on a specific topic, and they create your "worldview" on that topic.

All of the spells, beliefs, rules, values and paradigms related to "What I Am" make up your Identity. They guide your behaviour about relating to others and the world.

And, above it all, all of your beliefs, rules, values, paradigms and your Identity cluster into your Masterspell, which is your Core Paradigm. Your Core Paradigm is the sum total of "everything you think and believe that you know".

And it prevents you from EVER being able to see, access, experience and alter "What Is".

It is shocking to realise that the vast majority of what we think and believe and "know" is utter, complete bulls***. All of it is purely the result of spells that we "bought" along the way, and which now dictate our lives, our circumstances and even our available responses to those circumstances.

*"What is the outcome of all of the spells
in our lives?"*

- We endlessly experience the same pains and frustrations

- We automatically judge people and things and alienate those closest to us

- We find ourselves in "the same relationship" again and again even with "new" partners (same experience, just a different face), business and/or personal lives.

- We begin to feel confused and wonder if we might secretly be crazy, at least on "x topic"

- We begin to feel hopeless and powerless not knowing how we "got that again"

- We blame anything and anyone (Because we can't find the "hidden" cause, we feel certain that it must be something outside of ourselves)

- We decide we must have "lessons" to learn, and from this 'focus", we create an endless string of more and more lessons never knowing how to make it stop

- The "lessons" spell keeps us frozen in the belief that there "must be" a "Lesson Giver" up in the sky wanting to zap us every time we screw up.

We find ourselves trying approach after approach to change things but find the boomerang coming back again and again.

We can't figure out why this keeps happening over and over and over, and this is where we get that feeling of being totally stuck.

As an important side note: It is no secret that getting and having enough money is widely seen as the biggest challenge for most people in the world. Reading what you have read so far might lead you to believe that "money spells" are the issue.

Surprisingly, they almost never are.

Through working with thousands of people ranging in age, sex, race and culture, I have found that there is actually no such thing as a "money issue". It nearly all roots down in "***deserve-ability, and love-ability***" related spells.

That's why you can take every course on money, business, and success known to man. Yet, if you have a huge magnet inside of you that says, "I can't have", "I don't deserve", or "If I get, I suffer", you will stay stuck until you break that "spell", and change that paradigm.

The good news is when you break your "spell," everything changes instantly around that "spell.", and the better news is that YOU can break your spells - YOURSELF!

"How can I identify and get rid of my spells?"

Keep reading this book, as I'm going to a give you a powerful set of simple techniques, to dissolve your spells.

As far as identifying your spells, the good news is that you never actually have to do this.

I personally invested between £15,000—£25,000 on multiple belief elimination programs and systems, and I gradually came to realise that it was largely a waste of time, energy and money. Not to say that belief elimination (finding your beliefs and eliminating them), doesn't work; it can.

Yet, the reality is that we have potentially millions, or even billions of beliefs running through our energy and bodies. To find them all and eliminate them would take forever, probably about the same 13-15 billion years we took to create them.

More to the point, though, it's very rare that any belief related to a topic is what is actually causing our results in that area of life.

Usually we have hidden beliefs about other disjointedly-connected things regarding our deserve-ability, our love-ability, that cause these problems, so I don't waste any time identifying the spells and I wouldn't recommend you do either.

"Will one Spell-dissolve solve all my problems, forever?"

Breaking even one spell can create massive, wide-ranging, long-lasting results in one or more areas of life. A challenging reality, though, often arises after a powerful Spell-dissolve:

When one spell is broken, especially if it is a central spell (spanning multiple life areas), the next related spells rapidly arise to be met and dissolved.

Again, we have layers and layers of spells, hierarchies of spells. These spells create beliefs. The beliefs constellate into higher levels of spells, which we call "rules" and "values". All of the spells, beliefs, rules and values about "what I am" becomes our Self-Image Spell or "Identity". And, finally, ALL of our beliefs, spells, rules, values and identity makes up our Core Paradigm Spell.

When I do a Spell-dissolve session with a client, they invariably experience a radical, instant, deep and lasting shift into freedom, ease and grace in one or more areas. The larger the shift, the more freedom, ease and grace and the more related spells show up to be dealt with.

This often leads to me working with them more intensively to dissolve all of the spells relating to an area of life or, sometimes, doing an intense-multi-day transformation session. At the end of the book, I'll share more of the options available to you if you want to go further working with me.

Testimonial

"I had no idea how much I was fearful about being visible on social media, it would always put me in a funk every time I went on it to post, or comment on someone else's feed. Since Spelling breaking and Music Soul Journaling. I feel GREAT, Thank you"
Phillip Davies – Songwriter – Perth - Australia

****

Remember to join the FACEBOOK group as it's a community and support systems, that will help you on your journey to consciousness, and accelerating your success with like-minded indie singers and songwriters and my team. Share with us your revelations, your questions, your queries, and your breakthroughs: Accelerate Your Success Indie Music

Not on FB and have a question for me?
Ask by visiting www.beebyleighmusic.com.
I'd love to hear from you.

CHAPTER EIGHT
Shifting Core Paradigm

"What Creates the "Illusion of Problems"

Everyone has things in life that they really, really want that they seem unable to get. Things that, no matter what they do, seem to stay just out of reach.

You have one or more of these, or you would not be reading this book. So, let's reflect for a moment. What is one of yours? Maybe it's being signed to a publishing company, the extra zero (or couple of zeros) at the right end of your bank account balance, or perhaps singing at a specific venue…

Similarly, everyone has things in life that they really, really don't want. Things that, no matter what they do, seem to keep coming back.

Like the constant rejection "no" replies from playlist curators, publishing companies, record labels, or even sync agencies, or those signed contracts that are never in your best interest, earning little to no royalties from your songs or talent, making it more a hobby than a career.

Or maybe the same collaboration partners, or relationship partners keep coming back time and time again just with a different face, or maybe it's the living situation that always shows up again a few months after you relocate.

"Do any of these relate? What keeps showing up for you?"

What if I told you that ALL of these things were caused by ONE thing? One hidden cause? One invisible *"core constraint"*.

One of the promises of this book is that I will help you dissolve the "Illusion of Problems." What could I possibly mean by that?

Well, what if there was ONE issue, one hidden core constraint that was causing ALL of your problems? (Or, more accurately, causing the "illusion" of your problems.)

What if that ONE hidden core constraint was the reason why some of the things that you really, really DO want stay out of reach no matter what you do?

What if that ONE hidden core constraint was also the cause of ALL of the things that you really, really DON'T want, that keep showing up? Incredibly, it really is true.

I'll show you how it is true in a very unusual way

I'm going to introduce you to a powerful, practical, foundational business concept known as the Theory of Constraints (TOC).

Many years ago, I stumbled across this idea, which many leaders hail as one of the most powerful business concepts ever discovered.

The TOC is incredibly complicated and there are thousands of pages of information you can study and investigate.

For our purposes, I've distilled it down into a really simple, very powerful example that will illustrate my point:

Imagine you want to win a songwriting competition

You did everything possible to prepare to do so.

You studied under the best songwriter in the world for the last 5 years. You practiced singing every day to hone your voice. You bought the best guitar and took care of it meticulously to ensure it's always in top condition.

You wrote the best song you could and rehearsed it countless times.

You dressed in your finest outfit, confident and ready to perform. You had a nutritious breakfast to fuel your voice

The stage is set, and you've spent the last 3 hours meditating and visualising yourself winning the competition.

You've literally done everything you can possibly do to condition and prepare yourself to win.

"What are your chances?"

There's only one problem:

You have paralysing stage fright!

One tiny detail. And now, the question again:

"What are your chances?"

Sheesh! Even the other singer on stage is going to outshine you in this competition.

The theory of constraints shows that you can do all the best possible preparations, and you can fine-tune every possible practice, but if you have a major bottleneck at some point, if you have a significant constraint within your energy, nothing can positively impact your results as much as the removal of that constraint.

Another key idea of the TOC is that you can waste a lot of time, money and energy doing more preparations, and taking more courses, and more programs, and more singing or songwriting practice, and more drilling "victory" into your mind, (or, perhaps more self-help programs) etc. Yet, until you move the constraint from your energy, you're really just wasting your time.

Do not gloss over this, please, for your own sake. If you reflect on it for a moment, it leads to a massively powerful, freeing and very exciting truth.

If you have been "stuck", no matter how long you have been stuck, you can simply find and remove your Primary Core Constraint and you'll be able to move. Now, and Today.

It gets even better! When you finally remove your core constraint, all of a sudden, all of the time, the energy and money that you've invested in training, preparing, and visualising, all of a sudden, all of that comes to life and is multiplied in value.

This is true of any constraint you might identify and remove.

However, when you shift your Core Constraint, everything can change at once. Specifically, when you shift your Core Paradigm, ALL of the personal development, energy work, self-help programs and goal-setting work is all activated and brought into power in that moment.

Testimonial

"I was pretty skeptical about how one thing could change everything. Today, I am your biggest fan Beeby. Everything changes. I mean, my business, business bank account, my relationships, my creativity, EVERYTHING.
Ruth Berhe – Singer-Songwriter - Edmonton - Canada

So, what does this TOC (Theory of Constraints) stuff have to do with spells and energy alignment, becoming a Conscious Creator and personal-financial freedom? I'm so grateful you asked, because that is where we are going next.

It is time for a big shift away from what we "knew" to be true.

In the next few pages, you'll discover how to intentionally manifest and how to directly, consciously on purpose create and manifest everything you want to experience. (And how to stop manifesting what you don't).

What if you had a belief, a core belief, that was holding you back and you didn't know what it was? What if that belief, paradigm or spell made you unable to see "truth" by pretending to be the "truth"?

- You would experience a set of incomprehensible life experiences.

- You would find things that you have pushed away continually coming back.

- You would find things that you desire continually eluding you.

- You would seem to be powerless to change them.

- You would frequently catch yourself "doing it again", acting in a way that makes no sense to yourself or to others.

- You would make a resolution on New Year's Day and then find yourself making it again 365 days later.

- You would feel like a victim of circumstance or of "fate".

- You literally would not be able to see or understand what was holding you back because you were living in that paradigm, and you would be as oblivious to the hidden core paradigm as a fish is oblivious to water.

Does this situation seem familiar to you? Maybe a little bit?

The minute that you accept the possibility that there might be one core hidden constraint. One constraint that's actually causing everything you don't want to show up and causing everything you do want to stay away, you've got to ask the question.

"What is my hidden Core Constraint?"

Here is where your "Timeline Life Map" that you did in exercise two (2) at the end of chapter two (2) will be able to help you with the answer to the question "What is my hidden core Constraint?" "What is the overarching theme?"

Take your Timeline Life Map, and the answers to your four questions on each entered milestone, and see what core constraint (core theme) has created a pattern along your negative milestones timeline.

For example: A core constraint for me was a "lack of trust", causing the universe to repeatedly present situations that challenged "trust", leading to unfavorable outcomes regardless of my level of confidence or preparation for important events, relationships or those milestones.

The Power of a CORE Paradigm Shift

When I talk to people about what I do, I often run into initial skepticism. Many people just can't imagine how changing "one thing" can begin to create change in every area of life at once.

Yet, believe me IT CAN (I've done it in my own life too).

When you change your CORE (or central) paradigm, which is the Master-Spell that contains every issue that's holding you back, of course everything begins to shift to meet the awareness it brings.

Before we go off all the way into this, let's get a bit clearer on paradigms.

"What Exactly Is a Paradigm and What Is Your Core Paradigm?"

A paradigm is a way of seeing the world on a specific topic. It's a filter your mind uses for that topic. It dictates what you can see and think and experience on that topic. (More on that in a moment, when we begin to talk about the nervous system component known as the "RAS".)

A topical paradigm creates and dictates all of your thoughts, ideas, beliefs, experiences—all of your results on that topic.

Your Core Paradigm is the summary, the composite of ALL of your paradigms on every topic.

- It dictates and creates everything you can see and think and experience on every topic.

- It creates and dictates all of your results on every topic.

If that sounds far-fetched to you, just hang on and observe.

Remember our discussion on spells in a previous chapter?

It creates and dictates all of your results on every topic.

Each of us were born into a culture that is under the influence of a massive number of spells. Our culture includes our parents, our religion, and our school system of which programmed us to embrace different spells; and of course, we believed them.

Our Core Paradigm is the combination of all of those spells, a massive "Master-Spell".

As I said, for reasons we are going to see in a moment, your Core Paradigm, or your Masterspell, dictates everything you will ever experience, without exception. This ties to a point I made earlier and asked you to really take note of:

There is no continuity other than what we think and believe that we know.

Those things you don't want that keep coming back are the fruits of your paradigms.

The things you do want that stay out of reach do so because of your paradigms.

So the bottom line is this:

If your life is not the way you want it to be (remember our Theory of Constraints), you can work on everything, your practices, your skills, your behaviours, your potentials, and everything else, while experiencing little to no results, or temporary, short-lived results.

Because of this, nothing is more critically important than changing your paradigm, breaking that "**Master-Spell**" and releasing that Core Constraint.

Nothing will create the magnitude of results, and nothing will match the speed of results of addressing that over-arching Master-Spell.

****

Remember to join the FACEBOOK group as it's a community and support systems, that will help you on your journey to consciousness, and accelerating your success with like-minded indie singers and songwriters and my team. Share with us your revelations, your questions, your queries, and your breakthroughs: Accelerate Your Success Indie Music

Not on FB and have a question for me?
Ask by visiting www.beebyleighmusic.com.
I'd love to hear from you.

EXERCISE EIGHT

Learn How To Become Centred "In Your Power by Breath"

This techniques that I'm going to share with you. You can use at any time. You can use all the time. It will actually help you to be centered in your body, in your center of awareness, and in the center of the present moment.

The Multi Level Breath Technique

Before you begin, I want to offer you a word of encouragement:

This breathing technique, by itself, is actually enough to begin to transform your life and end the cycles of pain, frustration and chronic, unpleasant emotion for you. There is no way that I could overstate or exaggerate this.

The vast majority of people are breathing at a severely inadequate depth, and giving their bodies only a tiny fraction of the life-giving magic and energy of oxygen/air. The effects of this "normal" breathing are truly damaging and devastating in many ways

For our purposes, the main reason we are advocating this breath technique is because oxygen is the catalyst for fire;

including emotional fire. Deep breathing rapidly moves trauma, frozen energy and emotions out of the body. Later, when we get into Spell-dissolving, this breathing technique will be one of your greatest allies.

Multi level breathing done right, is the "life force" carried by the breath that brings healing and vitality to the body.

In Hindu philosophy including yoga, Indian medicine, and martial arts, the term is "prana," and refers collectively to all cosmic energy, permeating the Universe on all levels. Prana is often referred to as the "life force" or "life energy".

Before you begin, I want to bring your awareness to two concepts:

1. This breath technique is very basic, yet it does assume that you have familiarity with "Abdominal Breathing".

2. Most people in modern societies are not familiar with the true functions of the diaphragm or with the full process of breath in the body. Even many singers do not utilise their diaphragm fully.

Step 1: Breathe with Nasal Inhalation and Mouth Exhalation
First of all, using abdominal breathing, you're going to begin to breathe in through your nose and out through your mouth. As you inhale, bring air all the way down to your belly (so that your belly protrudes out, like a pot belly); and as you exhale, have it leave your belly fully (so that your belly returns to normal). You're going to practice that for several breaths.

Step 2: Make Inhalation and Exhalation the Same Duration
The second level of this breathing technique is to make sure
that the duration of your inhale and the duration of your
exhale are approximately the same length. We're going to
breathe in through the nose, out through the mouth and for
about the same duration with each phase.

Step 3: Expand Airflow The third level of this technique is to
begin to breathe in a little bit more deeply than you normally
would and breathe out a little more completely than you
normally would. When we breathe in more than usual, we're
going to be conscious of our diaphragm, as it comes down
and stretches our lungs. When we breathe out, our
diaphragm pushes our lungs up higher and pushes more air
out.

Step 4: Iron the Breath The fourth level of the breathing is
that we're going to imagine that we have an iron, like an iron
that you would iron your clothes with. We're going to iron
over the breath, so that it's smooth and continuous, with no
pause or gap in between. So as we breathe in and out, the
iron tracks over the breath and irons out all the wrinkles.

In effect, what we have now is a smooth flow of air coming in
through the nose and out through the mouth. We have an
equal duration of in breath and out breath. We're breathing in
a little bit more than usual, causing the diaphragm to go
down lower and come up a little more than usual, removing
more air. We can hear it and feel it. And then with the ironing
metaphor, we are also making sure that the breath is smooth
and continuous, with no gap or pause in between.

Step 5: Bring Love In with A Smile The fifth level of the breath is to actually bring a smile of love to your face. You may feel funny or weird or self-conscious as you do this, but it doesn't matter, just try it on anyway!

As you feel the love and you put the smile on your face, you are doing the only two necessary "practices": smiling and breathing.

Up until now, we have been pretty convinced that the way life works is that things happen, and we get happy and then smile, and there is some truth in that.

Yet it's equally true that those wires also run in reverse. In other words, when you smile, you send the signal to your nervous system, and to the universe (which is the rest of your body) that all is well, and helps to calm all your systems down, bringing you to a center of resourcefulness.

As you breathe in through the nose, out through the mouth and follow this process, you are adjusting and balancing your nervous system. You're calming your mind, your heart, hara, and your energy bodies down.

This will bring you into a more peaceful, calm and resourceful state. At the VERY least, because you're focusing your awareness on the breathing as much as you are, you literally cannot focus as much on those old limiting thoughts and patterns as you were before. Without attention, they begin to deflate like an unplugged inflatable toy.

If you are have problems breathing in general, please see a doctor. My official legal disclaimer can be found in its appropriate place in this book and on my website.

"Beeby, How can something as simple as breathing change my life"?

Many people asked me this question, but then they are stunned and amazed when they first discover the incredible healing and transformational power of conscious breath. I have come up with an analogy that has helped a lot of people to get this, so that they could integrate it into their lives.

Imagine a problem in your life. Maybe it's a money "block" or maybe it's a disease or a relationship issue that just keeps coming back over and over again, no matter what you have done to combat it.

In my work, I've discovered that all of these issues arise from frozen energy. Basically, chunks of energy frozen in the physical body. In my intense one-on-one and group work, I actually help people to dissolve those frozen chunks of energy at the root, freeing up tons of vital life force energy, and causing instantaneous, deep, and lasting life transformation.

So, for this example, I'm going to liken this frozen chunk of energy to a sandcastle.

Imagine that, while the tide was out, you have built the best sandcastle in the world. It is tightly packed, compacted, and then re-compacted until it's almost like solid rock. Looks and feels like solid rock. A sandcastle that seems just as hard and impenetrable as a brick.

You might think this sandcastle is indestructible.

And then the tide starts to come in. The mild wash of even the very first wave begins to demolish it. By just the third or fourth wave, it's all just sand again.

All that energy that seemed so stuck and solid, has now returned back to its original formlessness.

In this analogy, the sand sculpture is the traumatic issue and the frozen energy in your body, and the waves are your conscious breath.

As you breathe in and breathe out deeply, bringing in the healing power of oxygenated life force in and out, over and over again, while you're focusing on the feelings of that issue, you are actually, literally dissolving that frozen energy at the roots.

Once you learn to breath in this way, you will be able to breath more deeply while singing, which in turn will improve your vocal range, and expand the length in which you can hold a musical note for too.

GO DEEPER
Want some more help and support?
Visit www.beebyleighmusic or email
beebyleighmusic@outlook.com

CHAPTER NINE
Focus On Desired Experiences

Now that you have begun to shift your core paradigm, now that you are beginning to use your breath to release the frozen chunks of energy that were holding you back, and now that you are have begun to get centered and present in the new Paradigm, now what?

What flows from the acceptance of the possibility that you are an Infinite, Limitless Being, projecting out of time and space to have an experience?

All of the infinite wisdom, knowledge, information and power that's ever been and that will ever be is flowing out of eternity and into time and space through you.

And you are relearning that you have the full ability to focus all of that infinite energy with your mind and heart.

The wisdom, power and grace that creates universes is your nature. It is at your command.

Up until this moment, you have been creating your life, your world, and your universe unconsciously out of your spells. You were unknowingly allowing your inexhaustible flow of infinite power to flow from your spells into manifestation of more of the same.

What would it be like to stop creating by default, and to begin to consciously focus that energy explicitly into that which you want to experience?

I share with my clients and event attendees the Radical Truth of Infinite Intelligence:

1. All of the Knowledge, Wisdom, Information and Power that has ever been and will ever be is flowing to you and through you, at your command.

2. The only thing you cannot do is turn it off. It is going to continue to flow.

3. You've only got 2 choices of what you can do. You can either:

a) focus on what you want to experience or b) you can fall into thought.

"What Is The Outcome Of Falling Into Thought?"

When you fall into thought, you end up doing what the vast majority of us have been doing our entire lives, falling into the improper use of the mind.

We have access to all of the infinite wisdom, knowledge, information, and power flowing into us at all times like a fire hose, and yet instead of directing it to consciously create the life of our dreams, we are used to just letting it spray wild and willy-nilly all over the place, beating the hell out of us in the process.

When you fall into thought, you look at "what is" (or your "spellbound" interpretation of what is) and you think something like, "Aw, s***… this!"

Then you refer to memory and you look at all the things that that reminds you of the things we have already associated unconsciously with what is in front of us. And we give a second, "Aw, s***… this reminds me of that!"

With our focus on "what is" and "what was", we are unconsciously aiming the "Infinite Firehose of Creation Power" to spray into the formation and creation of "more of the same", and that's why things keep repeating.

Whenever we get triggered or begin to feel an unpleasant emotion around anything that's going on, the general habit is to think "Aw, s***, 'this' means 'that'". The minute that that happens, know that you've fallen into thought again.

You have fallen from Infinite Being and gotten stuck in your mental body, and you're going to be completely resource-less.

On the other hand, when you focus on what you want to experience, you actually take control of "The Firehose of Infinite Creation Power" through the lens of your mind and begin to consciously direct it (or "aim" it) into forming and manifesting what you want.

Focusing on What You Want to Experience

You've already mastered falling into thought, so….

Instead of doing more of that, I invite you to grasp the reins of your mind and aim that amazing "lens" to intentionally focus all the infinite wisdom, knowledge, information and power that's ever been and will ever be directly into what it is that you want to experience.

Now how, exactly, do you do that?

It's actually as simple as asking a question.

Well, not just any question. Many questions are downright destructive.

To begin to aim the Infinite Power consciously, we are going to ask Quantum Questions.

We will discuss Quantum Questions more in the next chapter, however for now we want to get you into action with a basic understanding.

A Quantum Question is a tool that literally aims and directs and focuses all of the infinite wisdom, knowledge, information and power that has ever been and will ever be, directly into the creation of what you are thinking and feeling about.

When you ask a Quantum Question, you do not go into your head and try to "figure out" the answers. Rather, you tune in and "feel into" the energies that arise in response to the question.

(You might want to read that again.)

An ideal Quantum Question to ask when you want to focus on what you want to experience would be: **"What would I like to experience now?"**

Let's take a moment, and take that in, and let's consider our first three keys:

Key 1: Consider the New Paradigm: "Infinite Being" projects out of Eternity into Time and Space to have experience. And it all arises and passes away a septillion times a second, so you are in a state of perpetual grace. There is no continuity other than what you think and believe that you know.

Key 2: Close your eyes and breathe deeply in through the nose and out through the mouth.

- Make the duration of inhale and exhale the same.
- Breathe just a bit more deeply in and out than usual.
- Iron out the wrinkles and really smooth out the breath.
- Smile and Feel the Love.

Key 3: Now, from inside of your body, not your head, ask yourself that question slowly, out loud:

"What would I like to experience now?" And feel into it. Feel your mind and your energy all calibrating and focusing itself to align with that question.

Don't try to figure it out, don't let the mind get "realistic," practical or logistical, rather just feel into the energy of that question.

> *"I'm not into the "woo-woo" fluffy stuff and I was a bit skeptical. Somehow, Beeby was able to help me, in one session, to find and rid a major life issue that had been holding me back, that I didn't even know I had!*
> *Beeby is THE lady who can help you, too"*
> **Jennifer Carter, Songwriter and Producer, BC, Canada**

GO DEEPER
Want some more help and support?
Visit www.beebyleighmusic or email
beebyleighmusic@outlook.com

CHAPTER TEN
Clear the Past (Spell-dissolve)

"Humans believe so many lies because we aren't aware. We ignore the truth or we just don't see the truth. When we are educated, we accumulate a lot of knowledge, and all that knowledge is just like a wall of fog that doesn't allow us to perceive the truth, what really is."
—Unknown

Now that we have begun to accept the New Paradigm, we want to fully shift into harmony with it. We want to stop re-creating more of "what is" by default, and we want to experience more of what we WANT to experience.

We are choosing to become fully Present and Centered, bringing our full resources of the New Paradigm into The Present Moment so we can effectively take the next step:

"Choose to Focus on What You want to Experience"

When you begin to focus on what you want to experience, you actually may find yourself moving directly towards it, and you might find it, actually "gasp"! happening for you!

There are going to be times when it's going to be very easy, even effortless!

And as you do this more and more, it's going to become easier and easier.

However, as I had said in a previous chapter, when you begin to go after something you really want, you will very often find your pre-existing related spells (and associated pains and chronic emotions) rearing their ugly heads and rising up between you and the experience you desire.

This leads us to a crucial, critical point:

And when you begin to move towards what you want to experience, you come face to face with everything you ever placed between "yourself" and "that" (which you are sure is "not yourself").

And it comes, again, with all of the chronic unpleasant emotion associated with the spells.

That's when it's time to do a Spell-Dissolve!

There are three types of Spell-Dissolves:

1. Basic Self-Spell-Dissolve
2. Full Self-Spell-Dissolve
3. Guided Spell-Dissolve

In form, they are similar.

In function, they are radically different. In truth, compared to a Guided Spell-Dissolve, the self-spell-dissolve are very limited, for reasons we will discuss in a moment. However, they can make the difference between heaven and hell in the moment.

Many people who get access to my book or free videos immediately know that this work is "for them" and that they want to investigate stepping to the next level with me, either 1-on-1 or in a group online.

If that is you, then you are going to experience one or more Guided Spell-Dissolve with me. Whether you feel that is true for you or not, I want you to have every resource possible for your own up-level.

Before we get into the how's, let's get totally clear on the why's:

"Why Are Spell Dissolving Necessary?"

As I said, there will be times when you will find yourself using the first three keys and just flowing with awesomeness.

Very often, though, the minute you begin to step towards what you want, you will find everything you ever put between yourself and that showing up, seemingly with the purpose of blocking your progress.

This experience can be intense. And the "bigger" your desire and the "bigger" the thing you are going after, the more intense the resistance.

And the more emotional-intensity carried in your spell, the more painful it will be to face it or experience it being triggered.

It will be helpful for you to get your mind "on your side", helping and supporting you with your desired outcomes, so let's get a clear understanding of exactly what is happening.

When you step towards what you want, you are doing a few things all-at-once:

1. You are creating change, which scares the hell out of your mind/RAS

2. You are moving towards something new, which also scares the mind/RAS

3. You are also going after something which, in all probability, is tangled up with multiple layers of beliefs and spells, which is going to stir up all of the emotions associated with the experiences during which the spells were created

This is a critical point: When we are triggered, the emotion that was tied up in the spell will be triggered. It will be one of our clues and allies. It will be the focal point we will aim our awareness at first.

1.   Basic Self-Spell-Dissolve:

This first Self-Spell-Dissolve can be used anytime, as a sort of "quick remedy" to getting yourself quickly out of a mildly un-resourceful emotional place.

It is in the form of what we had earlier referred to as a "Quantum Question." Recall that a Quantum Question is a tool that literally aims and directs and focuses all of the infinite wisdom, knowledge, information, and power that has ever been, and will ever be, directly into the creation of what you are thinking and feeling about.

When you ask a Quantum Question, you do not go into your head and try to "figure out" the answers. Rather, you tune in and "feel into" the energies that arise in response to the question.

When you begin to focus on what you want to experience and you notice resistance in the form of an undesired emotion, anger, sadness and/or fear, you can use this ultra-simple, yet deceptively powerful Quantum Question:

"How would I prefer to feel about this?"

And allow the question to resonate through your whole being…

In many cases, you will have a release and experience relief from this alone!

Why? Because you were unconsciously experiencing the unpleasant emotion of the spell and unconsciously focusing your energy and awareness there. The question itself is an effective wedge between your mind and your infinite being and it breaks the pattern very near the roots.

When the question alone doesn't bring relief, take the next step:

Feel into the unpleasant emotion and ask if it is anger, sadness or fear. (If you get any other answer, you are still stuck in your mind. You can easily move your focus back to your emotional body by asking again: "What emotion am I really feeling behind this story? Is it anger, sadness or fear?)

If you are having trouble with the answers you can use "The Sway" technique at the end of chapter four (4) to clarify your answers, using your body sway.

Once you know the answers, ask your Quantum Question again:

"How would I prefer to feel about this?" You will begin to feel the opposite emotion from the one you were stuck in. If it was fear, you'll begin to feel confident, certainty, safety or peace.

If it was sadness, you will feel happiness/joy arising.

If it was anger, you will find loving peace arising.

This Basic Self-Spell-Dissolve is the go-to tool for when the unpleasant emotion and resistance are subtle.

2. The Complete Self-Spell-Dissolve

In the Complete Self-Spell-Dissolve, you will delve deeper and you will more thoroughly dissolve the issue/spell that is blocking you, at its very roots. It is recommended to be in a safe, quiet, private, and unrushed space to do this so that you can be fully present.

Think about the issue that is blocking you. Really reflect on it.

You're going to begin to feel an emotion arise, and you're going to ask yourself two simple questions –

"What am I really feeling about this, is this anger, sadness or fear?" and "Where am I feeling the strongest sensation in my body?"

These questions are going to bring you out of the universe that's seemingly "out there". It will bring you out of your "universe body" focus, beyond your mental body and directly into your emotional body. Once you give awareness to the anger, sadness or fear, you're going to consciously feel the emotion, and you're going to allow yourself to feel it as completely as you can.

**Hint: The more powerfully and fully you allow yourself to really feel that emotion, the more efficiently and effectively you're going to dissolve the very roots of it. It is literally going to dissolve and depart from your body.

You will feel either a tightness, a tension, a constriction, a pressure, or even a pain.

As an alternative way to go deeper with "The Complete Self-Spell-Dissolve". Use the "Music Soul Journaling" technique that was exercise six (6) at the end of chapter six (6).

It would be quite understandable that you may require support to help you break the power these spells over you.

Further, the mind is blind to its own blind-spots. It's helpful and often necessary to have an objective 3rd party to help you see what you might not be able to see. I've provided the steps here because I want to give you the most powerful resources possible. Still, most people find that it's a whole lot easier, and a lot more powerful and effective, to have the Spell-Dissolve done "for them" by someone who is expert at holding the space, and helping them to stay present and focused.

3. Guided Spell-Dissolve

If you're presently experiencing something severe that you want help with, there are options for private 1-on-1, work with me. At the end of this book, I'll tell you about those options. For now, for whatever you're experiencing, be present with it. Feel it. Stay the course and keep reading, and we will see where you're at by the end of the book.

EXERCISE NINE

Indie Singer-Songwriter "Quantum Questions"

The use of quantum questions, also known as power questions, can be a powerful tool for keeping one's energy in alignment and manifesting desires. Quantum questions are designed to help you tap into the power of your energy and subconscious mind, and shift your perspective, aligning your thoughts, emotions, and actions with your goals and desires as if you have already received them.

When you use quantum questions, you're essentially re-programming your energy and subconscious mind to align with your desires.

These questions are formulated in a specific way, often starting with "Why" "what" or "how" and framed in a positive and empowering way.

For example: Instead of asking "Why am I not successful?" A quantum question would be "Why am I so successful in my music career?"

By asking these types of questions, you are training your mind to focus on possibilities and solutions, rather than problems and limitations. This can help you to shift your energy and bring you into alignment with your desires, which can ultimately lead to manifesting them.

It's important to note that manifesting your desires is not just about asking the right questions, it's also about taking aligned action and being in alignment with your desires. It's a combination of positive thoughts, emotions, and aligned actions that lead to manifesting your desires.

In summary, the use of quantum questions can be an effective tool for keeping one's energy in alignment and manifesting one's desires. It's a powerful way to reprogram your subconscious mind to align with your goals and desires, which can lead to positive changes in your life.

Here are a few examples of quantum questions that could accelerate success and abundance for indie singers and songwriters:

- "Why is it that opportunities are available for me to showcase my music and grow my fan base?"

- "Why is it that I have support with my career from the perfect team of industry professionals?"

- "Why is it that I am visible and gaining recognition in the music industry?"

- "Why is it that I have turned my passion for music into a sustainable and fulfilling career?"

- "Why is it that I was able to tap into my full creative potential and write hit songs?"

- "Why is it that I have built a strong personal brand and stand out in the music industry?"
- "Why is it that my live performances are awesome and I connect easily with my audience?"
- "Why is it that I was able to monetise my music and turn it into a profitable business?"

Keep in mind that these are just a few examples of questions you can ask, you can create your own set of questions that aligns with your specific goals and desires. The key is to make sure that the questions are formulated in a positive and empowering way and that they focus on already having received the outcome you desire (future forward), receiving possibilities and solutions, rather than problems and limitations.

Testimonial

"I have been repeating the same toxic relationship patterns for the past few years, and was feeling quite depressed and it was affecting my creativity and ability to grow my music career. Music Soul Journaling enabled me to see I was suffering low-self esteem and low self-worth within all areas of my life, since my parents divorced at the age of 5yrs old (30yrs ago). I feel invigorated and confident now."
— James Doughety, United States

Remember to join the FACEBOOK group
Accelerate Your Success Indie Music

EXERCISE SEVEN

"DISSOLVE STATEMENT" TECHNIQUE

This can help you to go deeper with "The Complete Self-Spell-Dissolve", as it removes everything hidden, stuck, trapped, and frozen within your energy. This effective technique can help you dissolve spells from any area of your life that you've identified in previous exercises at the end of each chapter.

Firstly: Breath in for count of 8, hold breath for count of 8 and release breath for the count of 8, to get you focused.

Secondly: Say the dissolve statement internally to yourself three times.

DISSOLVE STATEMENT

"I am ready, willing and able to unhide, unfreeze, unhook, un-attach, surrender my control, release, heal, dissolve and remove, all that I have identified as no longer serving me within my energy, and that I am now aware I have placed between me and my desires, preventing me from achieving success. I send all of it out into infinite possibilities to transmute back into energy, across all reflection that have been going into my reality, all universes, all times, all space, all dimensions, all planes, and all levels of consciousness and beyond, in the most easiest, joyous, and lovingly way."

CONCLUSION

The importance, and the power of continuing to work on your energy alignment and mindset approach throughout your music career and life is fundamental for achieving success as an indie singer and songwriter. As we go through different stages in our lives, we may encounter new challenges, obstacles, and opportunities that can cause us to lose alignment.

By understanding the power of your thoughts and energy, and by implementing the techniques and strategies outlined in this guidebook, you can dissolve fears and hidden blocks.

Many people find hiring myself or another coach or trained therapist for DEEPER energy alignments work, gets them to their end goal quicker. Yet, regardless of how you achieve your breakthrough, focusing on your inner game as well as the outer game of promoting and marketing your music, will accelerate your success to create a fulfilling music career, and a desired life.

REMINDER ON SELF CARE

Stay hydrated and get plenty of rest.

In some people; energy can release in a number of different ways from tiredness, cold like symptoms, burping, passing wind, yawning or in some very rare cases vomiting or diarrhoea.

These are normal side effects in some people and it just means that the negative energy has dissolved and you are in the healing phase.

Do not be alarmed if you have these symptoms or you if you do not, as everyone is different. However if these symptoms persist or are severe then contact your doctor.

ACKNOWLEDGEMENTS

I would like to say a huge thank you to the following people for their skills, help, advice, love and support

Louise Rook (Louise J Rook) for your patience, vocal, editing, narration skills, that brought this book to life.

Wendy Jacobs (Book Editing Service) for helping me proof read, and edit the content of this book.

The Publishing Spot Team (Alex) for helping me get my book uploaded to all the retailer, and online platforms to sell.

Lisa King (Valentine King Publishing) for your wisdom, advice and resources that made self publishing a breeze.

All my wonderful clients for entrusting me as your mentor, and allowing me to use your experiences and testimonials within this book to help others. You are all amazing!!

ABOUT THE AUTHOR

Beeby Leigh; is a British-Canadian award-winning singer, songwriter, lyricist, best-selling author, advanced practitioner in six different transformational change energy & mindset alignment modalities, and a mum to both her daughter and fur baby.

For more than six years; she has served fellow indie singer-songwriter clients, just like you, in permanently shifting limiting beliefs, blocks, fears, patterns and more that prevented them from being able to live the successful life they envisioned. With well over 2,500 energy alignment sessions, including several celebrities, she has grown to love working in the music industry, creating music, and serving her fellow clients.

Personally; she loves spending quality time with family and friends, travelling to new places, attending concerts, watching rom-coms, reading/learning, creative collaborations, long dog walks, and spending time near water (sea, ocean or lakes).

(AUTHOR) BEEBY LEIGH
Is Advanced Certified In These Energy Alignment Modalities

Emotional Freedom Technique (EFT-Tapping)

Matrix ReImprinting

Akashic Records

Energy Alignment Method

Colour Mirrors

HeartMath

MSJ Music Therapy

CONTACT INFORMATION

If you would like to work directly with Beeby Leigh in a 1:1 or Workshop to Accelerate Your Success, please contact

WEBSITES
www.beebyleighmusic.com

EMAIL ADDRESS
beebyleighmusic@outlook.com

Services Available Worldwide - sessions done virtually via
ZOOM VIDEO CALLS

Want to give feedback or give a testimonial on this book?
I'd love to hear from you.

MUSIC COLLABORATIONS
With Beeby Leigh

If you wish to work with Beeby Leigh in a music collaboration capacity, for Pop, EDM, Country or Sync Licencing opportunities, where Vocals, Toplines or Lyrics are required. Please reach out to discuss details via:

Instagram @beeby_leigh_music

Email beebyleighmusic@outlook.com

SAMPLES OF BEEBY LEIGH'S SONG TITLES
AVAILABLE ON ALL MAJOR PLATFORMS

Russian Roulette

When The Rain Came Down

Leap Of Faith

Epic Journey

Your Dreams

No Way Out

Warrior Dress - Change Is Happening

Beautiful Daughter

Lighthouse That Brings You Home

Only You

AUTHOR EVENTS
With Beeby Leigh

Although we cannot alter the past, we can work towards a brighter future by aligning our energy and leveraging the combined strength of sharing our experiences and the wisdom gained.

If you would like to book Author or Artist Beeby Leigh for your events, podcasts, interviews etc, please contact via:

Email: beebyleighmusic@outlook.com

Website: www.beebyleighmusic.com

With much love to you, Beeby Leigh xx

9 789696 928568